Happy On A Virgin's Island

Until I say, "I do," I don't and I won't!

By Crystaline Joi Prothro

Author of the potential bestseller,
I'm A Kid But I'm Not Kiddin'

A special section on secondary virginity.

Violation does not constitute loss of virginity.

HAPPY ON A VIRGIN'S ISLAND

Published by Robot Publishing Company
PO Box 961840 Riverdale, GA 30296
A division of JADOPRECRYS Enterprise

Cover design – Robot Publishing Company
Cover photography by Bob Johnson
First Printing – November 2000
Printed in the United States of America
ISBN 1-930505-02-7

TABLE OF CONTENTS

CHAPTER   PAGE

TABLE OF CONTENTS
(cont'd)

CHAPTER   **PAGE**

THE AUTHOR AND THE BOOK

Crystaline Joi Prothro is a vibrant 15-year old who already has one title to her credit, *I'm A Kid But I'm Not Kiddin'*, which she authored at age 13. This extraordinary bright young teenager has already begun to make her mark in the literary world. In her first book her focus was on child/ parent relationships and the extreme importance of parents and children learning to listen and respect one another. Her greatest emphasis is on the pressures experienced from being in a spiritual relationship with the Lord. The daughter of a very devout pastor, Crystaline shares her valuable insight on how compelling this can be. However, she yet encourages all young people to have such a relationship and to not be afraid to share with others their spiritual beliefs in God. Inclusive in her writings is a section where she shares statistics on the dangers of using drugs, alcohol and tobacco.

Chrissy is currently a student at Sandy Creek High School, Tyrone, GA. One of her goals is to maintain an "A" average throughout her high school career. Her dad loves to hear her say, "No, I'm not going skating today because I have homework to do," or as she said the other day, "Don't worry about the high 'B,' I'm going to pull it up to an 'A'." Her future aspirations include becoming a lawyer and an actress. She is the daughter of Pastor James and Donna Prothro.

Nominated *Author of the Year, Children's Non-Fiction Division* by Georgia Writers, Inc. and honored to be the very first recipient of the *Barry L. Taran Memorial Award* by Georgia Writers, Inc. for her first book has served as a motivating force to write this book. Chrissy is hoping that this new project will have an even greater impact. She has participated in several book signings along with radio and television interviews. In February 2000 she was recognized as one of Georgia's Young Black Achievers by 11-Alive News, Atlanta, GA.

In this, her latest release, she speaks on another social issue, *virginity* and its virtues versus the vices of *pre-marital sex*. Chrissy recognizes that the peer pressure that young people encounter to become sexually active during their adolescent years remains too high. The teen-age pregnancy rate and the statistics on STDs are alarming. Chrissy has refused to sit idle with no concern. It is her hope that speaking out on these issues, and more, will have an overwhelming impact on her peers as she writes on topics that few would dare to mention. *Happy On A Virgin's Island* is magnificent and a book that all young people must read.

Some of the greatest compliments that I have ever received have come from my family.

Dad,
"Chrissy, I Trust You!"

Mom,
"Chrissy, you remind me of myself."

My sister and mentor, Precious,
"Chrissy, being a virgin may leave you feeling lonely, but remember you're not alone."

My little two-year-old brother, Sir James Spēciál,
"I lub u Treesy! I get 'em fo messin wif u."
(I love you Chrissy! I'll get them for messing with you.)

7

DEFINITIONS

Webster's Third New International Dictionary (Unabridged) and Seven Language Dictionary

Virgin – A person who has not had sexual intercourse. Free of impurity and stain: not defiled; not yet disturbed; not previously treated or handled: as yet without contact.

Intercourse – Physical sexual contact between individuals that involve the genitalia of at least one.

Island – Isolate.

Isolate – To select from among others; to separate from all other substances: obtain pure or in a free state.

Diva – Goddess: prima donna

Prima donna – A person who finds it difficult to work under direction or as part of a team.

Happy – Having the feeling arising from the consciousness of wellbeing: joyous: blessed.

PREFACE

I believe that before we can deal with the issues of abortion, teen pregnancy, STDs, AIDS, etc. we will have to deal with the issue of *virtue* and *virginity*. As you read you will discover that virtue and virginity are two major components of this book. There are many people who are virgins from every race, creed, and color. To all of them I say, "More power to you and give God the glory!"

This book is intended to have an effect on the entire human race, not just the spiritual society. I do not apologize for being spiritual, therefore I do not apologize if the flow of this book is spiritual.

In no way could I, at 15 years old, have the knowledge and wisdom to write a book of this nature. I have solicited the help of many family members and friends under the supervision of Robot Publishing Company. These are my thoughts, feelings and sentiments written in a form that I feel will be beneficial to most of my readers. There is not one page in this book that I have not read, verified and therefore agreed with the principles that are suggested.

Thanks to all those who have contributed to getting this vital message out to a society that seems to have forgotten or misplaced the essence of *virtue* and *virginity*. To all who helped me and with my whole heart I wish to say, "May God bless you and may you stay happy."

INTRODUCTION

Hello. I am 15 year-old Chrissy, author of, *I'm A Kid But I'm Not Kiddin'*. *Happy On A Virgin's Island* is my second book and much credit goes to my biggest motivator and coach, Dad (also the author of several books). This book is somewhat different from my first one because it deals with the subject of *sex*. I have not intended to be overly graphic neither have I tried to play by the rules of the narrow-minded. As you read this book you will enjoy the story line of many virgins and non-virgins who have willingly shared their experiences in hopes that their scenario will be a teaching tool for others.

I have a variety of scenarios to share with you which include males concerned about their virginity (believe it or not), a couple who married as virgins, a 15 year-old who sadly regrets having sex, a woman who maintained her virginity until she was 20, a young male wanting to be different from his siblings by committing himself to one woman throughout their marriage (he takes pride in that he maintained his virginity until he married), a young girl raped of her innocence and coerced into having sex at the age of 11, and a special section from my mother who has been my example of virginity, having known only one man.

The subject matter of *Happy On A Virgin's Island* is *virginity*, a topic that has been all but buried in today's society. It was my mother who told me that the word *virginity* used to be a household word and it brought pride and self-worth to anyone that was classified as such. It is the intent of this book to revive the *virgin status* and to make it very clear that virgins still exist and we are happy about it. The stories that you read are real and tell about life experiences.

Moms and dads, brothers and sisters, grandmas and grandpas, and all other relatives will breathe a sigh of relief when they read *Happy On A Virgin's Island.* Here is written material that enhances a virtue that should be cherished by all people everywhere. Virginity crosses all prejudices whether it is racial, cultural, political, social, economical or religious. One topic that we can all agree on is that the practice of abstinence will make this world a much better place. It will help to reduce so many vices that are on the rise today, such as teenage pregnancy, STDs, low self-esteem and irresponsibility in our youth. In a world where "live for today for tomorrow we may die" seems to be the motto of the day, it is comforting to know that some things with moral implications are still being practiced.

I hope that I can encourage all of my peers to keep their heads in the books. First, I mean the Bible and secondly, educational material. Haven't we all heard that knowledge is power? Young men know this and that is why many will try to distract you from learning about the value of being a virgin. Education will keep you from being vulnerable to their "black book" tricks and games.

My editing team and I have not intended to manipulate the meaning of the definitions or change the statistics used through research to enhance or promote this book. There are occasions, for simplicity and/or clarity, that we may have paraphrased a definition or rounded off a statistic. As you will find, we are doing everything in our power to make this book powerful in its intent, acceptable in its reality, and comforting to all who read it. Thank you in advance for your patience and for allowing us to have a part in your life.

I do not know if I will ever write again. I know that if it is up to my father I will, so I'm hoping to have a great impact in the lives of all that will read this book.

THE GOALS OF THIS BOOK ARE...

1. To let you know that despite peer pressure and regardless of how old you are, it's okay to be a virgin.
2. To stress the need for morality, chastity and virtue, especially in my peer group. We seem to be losing these character traits at a rapid pace.
3. To introduce the concept of secondary virginity and to let you know that being a virgin can start again regardless of past mistakes.
4. To encourage my peers to read spiritual and educational literature above secular material that does not promote good standards.
5. To pat the backs of parents and encourage them to train up their child in the way that he should go (Proverbs 22:6).
6. To encourage more confessions of celibacy from virgins who may be hiding for fear of being mocked.
7. To heal past mistakes and evoke future aspirations.
8. To encourage the act of forgiving oneself.
9. To value the virtue of virginity instead of the vice of vanity.
10. To compete against the self-destructive vices of this society, i.e. drugs and alcohol, that impact the minds of today's youth. I hope this book will help young people to think in a more positive productive way.

V-I-R-G-I-N

Acronyms have been used for years to aid in the association of words and their meanings. Personally, I like them and thought that I should use an acronym for the word *virgin*. *Virgin* should be an important word among teenagers and the practice of maintaining one's virginity vital. Using the initial letters in the following words: virtue, intelligence, respect, genuine, innocence, and nonactive, I have created an acronym. Each word has been defined and its meaning simplified.

My intent is to compliment the person who is a virgin without insulting the person who is not. Therefore, I believe that my book is a joy to read and a fulfillment of a need.

OUR FRIEND THE ACRONYM

V **IRTUE** - To have virtue means to be pure, chaste, moral and innocent. It means you have stuck to your morals and standards and have not let anyone destroy them.

I **NTELLIGENCE** - The ability to creatively comprehend, reason and think. My personal definition of intelligence is making the right decisions. Keeping your virginity and staying pure is a right decision.

R **ESPECT** - To have esteem, honor or even difference. In this day and time I respect any virgin that makes the decision to be different. Some people think that it is abnormal to be a virgin. By remaining a virgin you are making a choice to be different and to respect and honor yourself.

G **ENUINE** - To be real, true, sincere and unaffected. This means you are not fake and you are willing to keep your body in its original state, which will leave it fresh and new.

I **NNOCENCE** - To be free from guilt or sin, chastity. Innocence is being found "not guilty" of having sex before marriage and therefore staying out of trouble with God. Innocence is easily detected by the older generation.

N **ON-ACTIVE** - To not have participated in any sexual activity, whether physical or mental. Proverbs 23:7 basically tells you that your mental thoughts determine who you are physically.

VIRTUE

Stick to your morals. Do not let anyone destroy them.
(Mom)

Virtue – morality and chastity (purity).

"... for all the city of my people doth know that thou art a virtuous woman." (Ruth 3:11c) How would you like for this to be your reputation in the community? This is what I really want for my peers and myself. In our local news broadcasts there are many stories about crimes that teenagers commit. How about "virtue" as today's main topic on the news? (Just a suggestion. Please don't get upset.)

The very first word in the *virgin* acronym is *virtue*. My dad, who is a "John the Baptist-type" preacher, has always told me to let my light shine. He says that I must do this from my mind and from my heart. Very simply, this means that making up the physical body to look a certain way does not make you virtuous. The way you think and the condition of your heart are vital to you being known as having virtue.

What if the community never saw with their own eyes, your misconduct and illicit behavior, yet they call you virtuous? Wouldn't you be living a lie and headed for trouble, especially if you did not correct the hypocrisy? To be complimented is to be responsible. If you want the compliments you should assume the responsibility of living up to what is being said about you.

If you are called virtuous then you have to be just that. If you were considered the smartest person in the class but you cheated on almost every test, you probably wouldn't feel right accepting the award of valedictorian. The same is true with being virtuous.

What about your dress code? Sometimes it's the way you dress that gives you the "no longer a virgin" image. To think that image isn't everything is to think foolishly. Our image should reflect our character, which is another lesson I've learned from my parents.

> **Being a virgin is personal but being virtuous is public.**

Being virtuous does not mean that you ought to distance yourselves from your peers although you have to still be careful of whom you hang around. My parents like to say that association brings about assimilation and I agree. If you are striving to be virtuous, expect those who are not virtuous to constantly try to persuade you to do what would prove that you are not virtuous. I think that you should be very careful about who you call your friends.

When I am in conversations with friends and they start talking about sex, or when I overhear conversations about sex, I'm glad that it's not me. Personally, I want to wait until I'm married to experience sex. There are just too many negatives to not waiting. One negative that stands out, to me, is the rumors that I hear about others who are active. I think to myself that was probably supposed to be kept a secret and never made public. Somehow it always seems to make the gossip hotline.

My parents are teaching me all there is to know about sex and life. I have at least come to grips with the fact that I do not need to experience a thing in order to make a responsible decision. I do not have to drink alcohol or do drugs to know that they are harmful. The same is true with sex. What else is there to make a virgin lose his or her most prized possession? I'm glad that I know some girls and boys that are virgins.

My dad thinks that every pair of pants that I wear is too tight. However my mom seems to be a bit more lenient and understanding. It is her words that I remember so often, "If you want people to respect you, you have to carry yourself in a respectful way." This means that you have to dress, talk, and act in a respectful way. If we reveal too much we must take responsibility when the question, "Why do you reveal so much?" is asked. "I don't know" is not a good enough answer. If we don't know we shouldn't do it. If we do things and don't know why we are doing them then we are just following the crowd and only God knows where the crowd will lead us. I'm desperately trying to follow my mother's footsteps and be virtuous and chaste until marriage. Since she has only known one man it is an honor to me. By listening to her, it doesn't take as much strength to remain a virgin as it does to maintain self-respect.

I don't know of any women more virtuous than my mother and my grandmother. That's where I get my desire to be virtuous. There is a lot of pressure out there, especially now that I am in high school. The boys are older and slicker (they think). They will cry on the phone, tell you how they want to take care of you (without a job), and they will even tell you they *love* you. This is soothing, no doubt, but not enough to rape me of my virtue and virginity.

With the divorce rate in this nation exceeding 50 percent, I'm very concerned about marriage. I do want to get married. My father tells me that what a man wants is usually not what he wants to give. He seems to want greater standards from his wife-to-be than he wants to give. Who said that a man could not be a virgin? That's who I would like to marry, a virgin. I know you're thinking to yourself, "Good luck girl."

> *When virtue meets virtue it will be much easier to maintain virginity.*

We seem to allow double standards in this society and it starts with our very own acceptances and allowances. Both, males and females, should have a standard, and maintain it no matter how handsome, pretty, or slick talking the other person is.

To all of my brothers who are virgins I praise you for your stance and want to compliment you on your courage. Do not feel alone. There is a lot of perpetration going on and I believe it's because of peer pressure. You would not be so pressured by your peers if you look at teenage pregnancy and abortion statistics.

INTELLIGENCE

Staying a virgin is the right decision.
(Crystaline Prothro)

Intelligence:
1. The ability to comprehend, reason, and think creatively.
2. Reflecting good judgement or sound thought (Webster).
3. Intelligence stresses success in coping with new situations and problem solving.
4. The ability to make the right decisions. These decisions are based on not what the consequences may be but rather on what is best for the individual.

    Many people think that being intelligent is being educated. Education is just not enough to help us in our determination to be a virgin. It takes sound judgment and sound thought. As teenagers, we need to take just a little more time to try to comprehend what is good or bad for us overall, and not just what feels good for the moment. I believe sex may only be a good feeling for the moment but it can lead to a lot of trouble in the future. Using our intelligence we are reminded that we are doing the right thing and making the right choice regardless of how bad and uncomfortable it may make us feel. If you were given the choice of ice cream or spinach, which would you choose? To be childish is to choose ice cream but to be intelligent is to choose spinach. I guess what I'm trying to say is it's not the good taste that we should want above good nutrition.

We all want to be friends with someone. I think it is a part of our nature. However, when and if one suggests that being friends means that we have to give up our most important virtue, virginity, then that friend is not a friend at all but an adversary. Knowing this is being intelligent.

> *My dad says, "Seldom does one marry the person that they lose their virginity to."*

Now that's something to be concerned about. I want to be like my mother, only one man all of my life. I'm not meaning to judge or "down" anyone else who may have already fallen into trouble with sex. It's just how I feel. To be intelligent is to reason and ask yourself the question, "Why should I take this chance?" Yes, having sex is a chance and a very dangerous one.

Just look at the startling statistics about sexually transmitted diseases beginning on page 139. These stats will never tell us how many gallons of tears have been shed because someone was disappointed and lied to. It's just not worth giving up your virginity on someone else's promises. What does that person have to lose? Nothing. When you lose your virginity it can make you feel like nothing.

My dad talks about the ego problem men have. He said they hate rejection from ladies and will try to do anything to get them to change their "no" to a "yes." They will, "...cry, lie and try," as he puts it. Can you believe this? They would literally cry tears to lure young ladies to have sex with them. My dad says it's only because they would like to have the pleasure of writing our names in their "black books" (this is a man's thing). It means scoring or let me say competing for who will be "king" by the number of times they have had sex. The who's who girls always score higher. I think this is so gross. I said to myself, "Is this all I am worth, a line in a book? I don't think so! I'm much more than that and it's my job to make that point very clear!" As I make my point I am respected for my stance.

Of course there are the *slickers,* the *players* (they call themselves), and God's gift to women. Many of them are virgins also (smile). They do not want to admit it because of peer pressure but sometimes their friends tell on them. Is it intelligent to perpetrate sexual activity for fear of being embarrassed? No it's not. But it is intelligent when we do not care what people think when we know their thoughts are negative. They may judge us for being virgins but it is perfectly alright because we are very proud to be. I have many friends and during rap sessions, while others may talk about having sex, we talk about maintaining our virginity. It is very intelligent to remain a virgin.

RESPECT

Self-respect is not scarred by someone else's disrespect. *(Dad)*

Respect - to avoid violation of your values and standards and any interference with them. It is the state of being regarded with honor and esteem.

   I must admit that I have heard older people say, "Respect is not something given. It has to be earned." In this day and time, earning respect will not be easy unless you really take a stand for good morals. We lose our right to earn respect when we start giving our trust and hope to people who only want to use us for selfish gain, like taking away our virginity.
   I have always been told that in the former generations respect was plentiful and gladly given, especially from children to adults. Children did not participate in grown-ups' conversations neither did they speak on

"grown folks" topics. Men were careful with what and how they said things when women were present because they did not want to show any disrespect to the women. You can really see this when you watch old movies or programs such as those on the Nick At Night channel on television. I must admit that many of them are corny but still they show the respect that people had for each other.

Nowadays, some men do not care what they say in the company of a woman neither do they care what they say directly to her. They walk up to us and say, "You are so sexy." (My big sister tells me that this with its sexual connotations should be considered an insult.) Where is the compliment in this kind of approach? There is none and they don't intend for there to be one. It is not your fault if you are perceived to be attractive, so please do not feel guilty because of another's disrespect.

Today's guys use profanity in the midst of girls and virtually talk about anything they please. To be honest the girls have a language as well. Back in the day men were taught respect and women demanded it. Things change and people do too. Respect goes far beyond saying "ma'am" and "sir." It also has to do with how, why and when we should respond to a given situation.

If a guy walks up to us and says, "Hey shawdy, can I come home with you tonight?" then he has said something disrespectful. "Shawdy" or "shorty" is another one of those disrespectful words. Calling a person "shawdy" is the same as addressing a person as if you know them when you know you do not know them or their name. The way we respond will determine whether or not we respect ourselves. We can choose to respond in a very lady-like manner or we can just walk away. Responding to that ignorance is allowing him to disrespect us. Don't disrespect yourself by responding to ignorance with another type of ignorance. We don't have to be dis-respected. Keep your self-respect.

Virginity alone does not automatically bring about respect. If we lie about our sexual activity or inactivity then we do not respect ourselves. If we are ashamed of being a virgin then we have disrespected ourselves. If we allow others' laughter, pressure or ridicule to make us feel bad for what we have chosen to do, we have lost respect for ourselves. I think we all should enjoy our virginity and respect our choice to be virgins. I have always heard from the experienced people that, "Men want the wild ones now and they want to marry the tamed ones later." This may be what they want but it is not what I want. I'm en-joying my self-respect. It feels good.

I truly believe that respect has a lot to do with how we feel about ourselves as well as how others view us. It's okay to want to look good as long as it doesn't become vanity. It's okay to smell good as long as the motive is right. Having and keeping respect for ourselves, both physically and mentally, will cause us to see that what others say and do is their way of life, not ours. What works for everyone else probably doesn't work for us. We must discover what helps us to respect ourselves and what helps to enhance and make us better.

When a person respects himself he will be given credit for having avoided violation. Refusing to let any-one violate our standard is very important. It proves that we respect ourselves. Self-respect makes us independent of other people's okay for our lives. If they agree with our morals, standards and virtues then that's okay but if not then that's their problem. I am sure that there are many who respect themselves and mean to keep it that way. In some cases it is the opposite. Many are prepared to re-spect themselves as long as their boyfriend or girlfriend does not demand that they give up their virginity. Usually things have gone too far if someone even thinks that they can ask us for what is so important to us. I truly believe that self-respect will go a long way. It goes along with being a virgin. Self-respect is one of the main reasons that I intend to maintain my position as a virgin. I respect myself, boy that sounds good especially when you really mean it!

I want to share another point of virtue. Do not let anyone talk to you about sex out of perspective. Seek advice about sex from your parents or someone who has your best interest at heart, not some egotistical person who only wants to bear the mark of being the one that broke you down. You cannot say that you have respect for yourself if you allow other people to disrespect you in conversation. I really believe that this is why parents do not like the idea of late night phone conversations. They can get out of control. You must keep them in order. Lose a so-called friend if you have to but keep your respect.

GENUINE

Our character should equal our conversation.
(Pastor Rosalynn Curry)

Genuine – to be real, true, sincere, and unaffected.

One of the words that define genuine is unaffected. When you are a virgin, along with being pure and untouched, you are unaffected, meaning you have not been influenced. By being a virgin, you are real, true and sincere to your body by letting it remain in its original state. Your body remains new and fresh.

Why is it so hard to just be yourself? I blame peer pressure. It almost pushes you to want to be someone else. Being genuine is not for other people but for you, especially since other people are so easy to fool. God is not easy to fool. As a matter of fact we cannot fool God.

Speaking of fooling people, let's talk about the word "diva." To be accepted by society as a diva is not what we think it is. *Diva*, in my opinion, is not a good word. It means a *goddess*. (How do we use the word goddess and not mean a god-type? The Bible says that there should be no other god before our God.) Society pumps up the idea of being a *diva* as if it is what we want to be. I wonder how many divas are virgins? **If being a diva does not mean being a virgin then being a diva is out!** I really believe that the pressure of maintaining that image will keep us from being genuine.

Wearing make-up can keep us from being genuine. We can get so used to wearing it until we feel ugly and insecure without it. At my photo shoot for the cover of this book, my dad was complimenting me and telling me that I was gorgeous and that he appreciated the fact that I had no make-up on. I replied, "Dad, I have make-up on but very little." Then he said, "You are just genuinely beautiful."

I believe that genuine beauty and talent is important. We must always remember who we are before we allow someone else to pressure us into being what they want us to be. I think that my sister is absolutely gorgeous (and silly I should add, sorry sis). She does not want me to ever try to be like her or anyone else. "Just be yourself," she says.

My dad is a renowned pastor but he will not let the compliments of being this or that push him into a "self" world. He says whatever we are, is known by God. No one else matters. Liking yourself is different than being "stuck on yourself." That can be a bad thing. However, all of us should be so genuine that we appreciate whom God has made us. We are all different but special to God and hopefully to our families.

I do not like people who fake and perpetrate. Why can't we just be real and genuine? I believe that we should say what we mean and mean what we say. It may not be popular with the crowd but it will keep us genuine. I wonder why so many so-called virgins will not say they are virgins before the world of skeptics? What's wrong with the world knowing that we are virgins? This book certainly puts me on the spot. Yes, I am a virgin and I'm glad about it. I do not feel like I have missed anything. I feel no pressure being a virgin and am glad for my friends that are virgins as well, both boys and girls. There are many of us. Peer pressure makes many want to hide the fact that they are virgins because of trying to fit in with the crowd, but that's not being real is it? When my mom talks about being with only one man, she seems so happy and it encourages me to want the same. If I marry (and I really do plan to one day) I want to have that same testimony.

People are good at saying little things to us like, "You don't know what tomorrow will bring." That's true but today I am genuinely glad to be a virgin. I try to keep my mind clean and honest. That's how I know I'm genuine. I hang with others who think just like me. I love the Lord above anything else and I have generational examples like my grandmother and my mom. This thing can be done and is being done. To all who will read this book, "Keep it real," and do not always trust "whatever is clever." It is better to live with never, or let me say until I get married.

INNOCENCE

Innocence = In no sense guilty *(Zondra Kurtz)*

Innocence – To be free from guilt or sin.

Innocence has a hanging partner called independence. To me, independence means to be who you are without the help of anything or anyone. Different people have their own reasons for having sex. For whatever the reason, I hope they realize that they can always be who they are without having sex.

Innocence is a big part of virginity. However, it does not mean that the one who is innocent is also naïve. Innocence simply relates to a chosen few. The appearance of innocence, the feel of innocence, the emotions of innocence and the results of innocence are rewarding.

The appearance of innocence is noticeable without a word being spoken. The experienced and the inexperienced can see the innocence of a virgin. When we walk into a room there are those who look up to us and then there are those who despise us. Some despise us because we are doing what they wish they could have done (remained a virgin). Others will despise us because they know that we won't come down from the standard of innocence. There is also another group that lie in wait for our blood. They are often referred to as vultures or dogs. (While I do not advocate the statement "all men are dogs", there are some men/boys with dog-like tendencies.) Be sure to be careful of them young ladies, because with our innocence they see vulnerability. *Being vulnerable is a part of innocence but we do not have to possess ignorance.* We are all vulnerable and susceptible to things in life. For some people sex is important. It is important that we can learn from young adults and see just how they handle the pressure as well as learn from those that are experienced and have stories to tell.

We probably won't be able to recognize the feel of innocence as often as others can see it. As young people, we may sometimes feel like outcasts because we are so innocent. Others, I'm sure, help to contribute to the feeling that we are missing something. Believe me, it is worth the wait. There are those that lie in wait for us and want to take advantage of our innocence. They do this because they know that there is a certain amount of vulnerability that comes when one is innocent. Please remember, young people, no matter what they say and how nicely they say it, this vulnerability does not at all compare to the vulnerability that comes once our innocence becomes non-innocent. Once you experience sex, your world of curiosity opens and ushers in vulnerability. Keep that feeling of innocence and there is a sense of accomplishment that you should receive every time you can say, "Yes, I'm a virgin." Be sure that you are never ashamed because others are looking at you and you are setting a very important example.

Emotions go up and down and are very confusing. They sometimes give false feelings and will make us think that what we feel is real. We should never allow emotions to make our decisions. Emotions will make you think that someone loves you when they really don't. Emotions can make you feel that it is time to have sex and it really is not time. *Those that lie in wait for our vulnerability also search for our emotions and they are artists at saying what they need to say to get us where they want us (in sexual submission).* Be strong and stand on your decision to stay on the "Virgin's Island."

There are positive results to maintaining innocence. The result of a clear mind is the ability to make A's. The result of inactivity is the saving of our bodies until marriage. The result of life will be our ability to pass on the good feeling of waiting to our children, just as my mother has done with me. Again, I must let you know that innocence does not necessarily mean that you are naïve but it does mean that you are special.

NON-ACTIVE

Actions speak louder than words unless the word is virgin. *(Precious Prothro)*

Non-active – To not have participated in any physical or mental, sexual activity.

    First let me say that "non" means none and not any. We are so ready to think this should only mean physically but I would rather associate it with mental and verbal as well. This means we should pay very close attention to what we say and what we allow to be said to us. We also need to be mindful about how and what we think.
    I have learned from my parents that the mind is a very strong machine. In Proverbs 23:7a we read that a man is whatever he thinks (paraphrased). This should really make us concerned about our mentality. When our peers start talking about sex, we should stop them right

away. They will not stop on their own. We all know what a conversation can make us think about and how strong the thoughts can be, so we will have to watch our thoughts if we want to be non-active. The title *non-active* could mean physically non-active but it is okay to be verbal or mentally active. I don't think that this is how we should take the word *non-active*. It means don't get involved in any way. All of it is harmful and can ruin our future. I really believe that sex is a mature activity and not just something to do.

When we have to be constantly told to clean our rooms, to turn off the television at two o'clock in the morning, and to not go out "half naked," then we should accept the fact that we are not responsible. Therefore we should not even talk, think, or try to picture sex in our minds. Having sex requires responsible thinking. It seems to be complicated. Let's just stay away from it. It's not time. Being *non-active* is just so safe. We won't have to worry about getting pregnant, diseases, abortions, etc. When we add it up, having sex is just not worth it. From what my friends tell me, and I think you will agree from the storylines in this book, sex is "not all that." I believe that the reason it is "not all that" is because it should not be taking place anyway. It is sin. It is wrong. It is dangerous and most of all I believe it is silly.

I wonder who gets the benefit out of having sex and giving away one's virginity? Most people would say the guy. My friends, who are upset with themselves for yielding themselves to sex, seem to agree that there is nothing, or let me say, very little in it for the girl. Is being part of a group worth it? Is it worth it just to have the right to say that you have had sex? Does this right make you feel good or bad? I would think bad.

I think that we should be proud to be non-active. You may not be a virgin but you can still be non-active. Your past mistakes are forgiven by the Lord so don't feel so bad about them. You can still be non-active and virtuous. It does not matter what other people think about you. God forgives and loves you. I feel so good being non-active. I do not want to sound like a judge and I really do not mean to if I do. I know that there are many who hate the fact that they lost their virginity. Being non-active is where you can start again. Make up your mind today that you are going to be non-active verbally, mentally and physically. I know that it gets hard but we can do it. Remember that non-active means non-pregnant, non-diseased and no abortions. Always remember WWJD (What Would Jesus Do). Jesus would be non-active.

LETTING YOU KNOW
By Crystaline Joi Prothro

Are you just following the crowd
Or are you just curious?
Is it something you think
Or know that everyone does?

I'm not sure what you heard
Or what you might have seen,
But as for me
I'm not with that sort of thing.

If you don't know what I'm talking about
I'm talking about being a *virgin.*
Now don't sweat me
You're gonna hear it again.

I'm sure you've heard it from your parents,
And from me you'll hear the same,
That this whole world of sex
Is nothing but a fool's game.

Although I'm young
And you may think this is rated X
I do know that the bible says,
Be married before having sex.

You may think you're ready
But I believe you would want to wait,
Because you want to start your marriage
With a new and clean slate.

Now, this book is about being happy
On a Virgin's Island that is.
But not just on "her" Virgin's Island
But also on "his."

GETTING AN UNDERSTANDING

By Crystaline Joi Prothro

Teens have already learned the difference
Between what's right and wrong.
To know they need to do what's right
And how to stay strong.

With all of the sex, violence, and gangs
That unfortunately, we are around,
It's hard to stay focused
And hard to be sound.

Sound in the word of God
Sound being intact.
Being able to read the Bible
And understand it at that.

You may not understand it all at first
Why you shouldn't lie, cheat, steal or curse.
But one thing is certainly your responsibility to do,
Stay away from unmarried sex; you know what it can do.

When you grow in the Word, it will all be so clear
If you will not only listen, but hear.
If the pressure of sex makes you not want to contain
Then pray for your mate and your virginity maintain.

Some people might say
That being a virgin is being "lame,"
But when they say that, you just say
That's better than playing the STDs game.

Having sex is too risky
You could end up with some disease,
So for the sake of your body
Just don't have sex. PLEASE!

INNER FEELINGS

By Crystaline Joi Prothro

What is this feeling?
What is this thing I feel?
Is it really here?
Is it really real?
I need someone to tell me what these feelings are
It seems no one can help me, everyone seems so far.
They seem so far away, they can't hear me when I scream
Am I really awake? Or is this all a dream?
Are these feelings good?
Are these feelings bad?
Are they supposed to make me happy?
Or are they supposed to make me sad?
Are these feelings right?
Are these feelings wrong?
Are they meant to make me weak?
Or are they meant to make me strong?
Will I get in trouble for these feelings?
Or will my parents understand?
Because my mother was once a young girl,
And my father had to become a man.
I'm sure they know about these feelings,
They had to have had them too.
These feelings are lonely and secretive,
But they're nothing new.
Many before us have already felt them
And conquered the stages of life,
So to all my peers and friends,
Hand your feelings over to Christ.

THE DECISION

By Crystaline Joi Prothro

You don't want to be called
lame,
And you want to be well
known.
You think that you love
someone
And you're afraid of being
alone.

I don't think you understand
Everything that could go
wrong
And in the end
You'll be singing a very sad
song.

A song of death,
Maybe a song of birth.
A song of another life
Being put here on earth.

Another life
That you're unprepared for.
Whining, crying
And a whole lot more.

Now you need to sit down
And think about what
you're going to do,

Because having sex may
have an effect
On more than just you.

If she gets pregnant
It'll affect the girl,
And if you get a disease
It could affect the world.

Your parents are affected
By everything that you do
Because they know that you
love them
And they love you too.

They only want what's best
For you and your life
That's why you should wait
Until you're pronounced
husband and wife.

They want to make sure
That you're living the right
way
That's why they watch over
you
Each and every day.

I'M NOT ALONE

By Precious Prothro

An island once full of people is now filled with pain,
Others are constantly leaving, still I must remain.

Less and less are the faces that I see,
Many left for a bogus desire to be free.

This can't be true, everyone can't be gone,
Why should being a virgin leave me feeling so alone?

What is that shadow I see coming my way?
I hear a voice saying, "I would like to join you
if I may."

Quickly I strain to see just who this might be,
Thank God it's others coming to the island
and they feel just like me.

On the values of our morals,
We have decided never to leave,
No matter who comes along and tries their
best to deceive.

Although sometimes we feel just a little out of place,
We have God to thank for this island,
That is filled with grace.

A DIFFERENT TYPE OF ALONE
By Precious Prothro

How I remember that feeling of being all alone,
Yet on a different scale, I was the first to be gone.
I looked back to where I'd departed from,
In hopes that someone else would also come.
I really didn't want them to hurt the way I had,
But out here was so scary, and I felt so very bad.
No longer a virgin, why was I the one taken,
My heart bled and oh was it achin'.
Is there any way I can go back to that special place?
Can I obtain that favor and be part of that grace?
With tears in my eyes and my head in my hands,
I heard the voice of repentance saying,
"You can fix it, I know you can."
If only it was that easy,
If I could turn back the hands of time,
I would stay on that Virgin's Island,
And declare that what's mine is mine.
So if you are there, stay there until it's right to leave,
Don't let anyone try and persuade you to depart,
For this is intended to deceive.
When they say you're crazy
And they look at you and laugh,
Just remember what you possess
And what great and special qualities you have.

JUST CHILLIN' JUST TALKIN'

As a couple of my friends and myself sat and talked about our views of being a virgin we came to the conclusion that we're not ashamed. We think it's a great accomplishment. At our school, boys and girls don't talk about their sexuality much. Usually the girls that do have sex do it because they think their relationships are going to last. Some kids have sex because of the peer pressure from their boyfriends or girlfriends. The media also has a part in the pressure on teenagers. They know exactly what we like to watch so they put a bunch of sex scenes in the movies but they don't show the scenes of the awful consequences, i.e. the babies, the diseases, and the loss of innocence.

In my neighborhood the guys know whom they can and cannot approach about certain things. My friends and I have never been pressured to do anything we didn't want to do. Then again that might be because of the way we carry ourselves. Although we haven't been pressured to do anything, we still know that because of the pressure that is out there that we have to be strong-willed and we can't be overwhelmed by our feelings.

In this day and time, as much as I hate to say this, oral sex has become more common among teenagers than actual intercourse. I guess kids think of it as sort of a replacement. I believe that they probably think that as long as they're having oral sex they're still virgins. Either way it goes sex is sex.

I think that it's so pathetic that some parents don't care what their kids do as long as they don't get pregnant, get anyone pregnant, go to jail, or end up dead. I guess they don't realize that these are the serious effects that could happen when their kids are sexually active.

DATING CAN BE PAINFUL

Different people have their own reasons for having sex. For whatever reason my hope is that they realize that they can always be who they are without having sex. In my age group, many teens are taking this time in their lives to say that they only have one life to live so they're going to live it like they want and when they get older they'll change or correct their lives to make them better. Well, I don't think many of them have really thought this plan through because they don't realize that once you've lost your virginity it is hard to regain it. (I'll explain later in my section entitled Secondary Virginity on page 133.) Mentally you may be able to be renewed or purified but physically you'll never be the same.

> *Independent is being intelligent. It means to be free of or having no need for outside control.*

At this time I would like for you to join me in a storyline that really expresses the importance of how our own independence survives off of what God has given us as individuals and not having to borrow from someone else who probably does not mean us any good anyway. It is so important that we are independent where our sexuality is concern.

Here is a story I would like to share:

Although I have never gone through a situation such as the one in this story and the incidents that I describe are totally fictional, I want to say something to those who are able to relate to it. By listening to my parents, I know that life gets better as you get older. When situations like this come about, since you can't turn back the hands of time, you can only pray, and hope for a better future.

When my parents said we were moving, I didn't think anything of it. When we finally got to our new house I knew my life was about to change. I didn't like the idea of changing schools. Something was different about this year. Maybe it was that I had just turned 16, maybe it was that I was in the 10th grade or maybe it was that this was my first time going to a co-ed school.

My parents had kept me in an all-girls school in both elementary and middle school. I never knew why but I did know that they always trusted me no matter what. They would tell me every day how much they loved me and trusted me.

It was the first day of school and I was so excited. When I got on the bus, right off, I made a friend. Her name was Nicole and she was a junior. Nicole was very popular and I felt like we would make good friends because we were both polite, friendly, smart and, to be honest, very pretty. Nicole showed me around to all of my classes and introduced me to all of her friends.

There was one friend of Nicole that really got my attention. His name was Johnathan. Although Johnathan wasn't the cutest guy in the school he was still very nice and sweet. He was also on the football team. I had always told my friends that if I ever had the opportunity to go to a public co-ed school I would definitely date a football player.

Nicole, Johnathan and I got to know each other very well. Everyday we would have lunch together. One day Johnathan finally did exactly what I was waiting on him to do; he asked me for my phone number and of course I gave it to him. I told him that I had to be off the phone by 9:30pm but he said that he did not get off work until 10:00pm. I didn't want to disappoint him and make him not like me so I would sneak on the phone and call him around 10:30pm. Something had to be great about him because I had never even thought about sneaking on the phone. I didn't want to lose my parents' trust.

One day at school Johnathan asked me to go the movies. My parents would kill me if I ever even thought about dating before I was 18. Well, once again I didn't want to push him away so I decided to lie to my parents. I made a plan to tell my parents that I was going to sleep at Nicole's house because they really liked her. Then we would have Johnathan and his friend Keith come and pick us up. Nicole's mom didn't mind her going out at any time of the night.

Just as planned Johnathan and Keith picked us up then drove us to the movies. While watching the movie I got kind of nervous because I knew what those "movie scenes" always looked like on TV and I wasn't sure if that was going to happen. I had never been this close to a boy in such a dark room. I didn't know how to act. Finally, he grabbed my hand to hold it. I wasn't sure if I was even ready to go that far but I didn't want to look like a little baby so I held his hand. Later he leaned to kiss me but I knew I wasn't going there.

The next week at school nothing had changed. Johnathan told me he needed to talk to me but couldn't figure out what he had to say. One night we talked on the phone (at this point I routinely snuck on the phone) and by the time I got off I had my very first boyfriend. The next day when I got to school Johnathan brought me some chocolates and flowers. I didn't think anything of it. I just assumed that that was some-thing boyfriends were supposed to do.

Soon it came time for the prom. I was afraid to ask my parents if I could go. Finally I asked because I wanted to go so badly. I had always dreamed of going to the prom, getting all dressed up, riding in a limo, and eating at a fancy restaurant. After about three days of thinking, my parents finally decided that I could go. We bought my dress and shoes, and set an appointment to have my hair and nails done. Nicole, Keith, Johnathan and I were going to have a great time.

Prom night finally came. I got dressed and went to Nicole's house and the guys picked us up from there. We went to the prom. We later left the prom to eat at this nice restaurant over on the south side. After the dinner the guys decided they wanted to go look at the stars in the park. Before we went to the park Johnathan said he left his music at the house. (I was blind not to see this coming.) He said he didn't want us to wait in the car so he told us to come on in. (By the way, his parents weren't home.) Johnathan took so long finding the tapes I thought I would go up and tell him to come on. Little did I know that that was exactly what he expected me to do.

He invited me into his room. Just as always he told me how pretty I was but he added that since we loved each other so much we should show it by having sex. I had always just pushed it away when he said it before but somehow this time seemed different. He actually sounded like he meant what he was saying. I never thought that I would be in this position. At this point I thought that I really loved him. Slowly I began moving toward him in a way that said "yes." He asked me if I was sure about what I was getting ready to do. I really wasn't sure but I knew that this night might be the last chance I would have with Johnathan. I felt a strong pressure of do or die. Johnathan was my first boyfriend and my first love; therefore, I wanted him to be my first where sex was concerned. So I took my immature thoughts and did what I wanted to do. We had sex. Afterwards Johnathan and Keith took Nicole and me home. It was about 1:45 in the morning.

The next morning I just knew that my parents would know what I had done. I felt so cheap and I was so ashamed of myself. I just kept hearing, in my mind, my parents' voices telling me how much they loved and trusted me. I slept really late because I got in so late. When I finally got up, all my parents did was ask me if I had fun at the prom and they wanted all of the details. Well, I guess you can figure out that I didn't tell them all the details. That would be dumb on my part. My mom spent the whole day talking to my grandmother, telling her how proud she was of me. She also told her that she was surprised at how well I was doing with adjusting to the new school and the new house.

When I got to school the following Monday it seemed as if everyone knew about what had happened to me on prom night. Everyone was giving me this look and making different comments. I didn't like this so I decided to confront Johnathan. When I finally talked to him I asked him if he had told anyone about what we did? We had promised each other that we wouldn't say anything to anyone, except for Keith and Nicole because they were our best friends and we told each other everything. He replied, "Baby I told you I wouldn't hurt you. Don't you trust me?" Although he did not directly answer my question, he sounded convincing.

The next weekend seemed to have come so fast. Just like every weekend Nicole and I made plans to go out with Johnathan and Keith. We would always go to the movies but this weekend Johnathan, for some reason, wanted to go and do something different. Now, I know that he wanted to do what we did before, have sex again. Because I didn't want to lose Johnathan, I agreed to come to his house. It happened again. This time I was really worried about what might happen to me.

The next morning I woke up and I was so sick. I mean I was throwing up everywhere and my stomach was hurting really bad. I wasn't sure if I had something or if I was pregnant. I needed to go to the doctor. I told my parents that I wasn't feeling good but, of course, I didn't tell them why. My mom took me to the doctor as soon as I told her I was sick because I wasn't sick often. The doctor examined me. He diagnosed me as having a bacterial sexually transmitted disease. He agreed to not tell my mother if I promised to take all of the medication that he prescribed. I certainly agreed.

I guess Johnathan assumed that I liked what we were doing so he wanted it to be a routine thing. He asked to make another date for the next weekend. I told him that I didn't want to do it anymore because, although I was lucky those first couple of times, I could end up pregnant. Johnathan said that he understood and didn't want to try and make me do what I didn't want to do. I never told him about my visit to the doctor for fear of losing him. Again, I felt like he really meant what he said. I actually thought that Johnathan and I were going to get married some day.

When the summer came and I was about to turn seventeen. Johnathan, Keith and Nicole told me about Keith's pool party that he has every year for his birthday. This was also the time when his parents would go on their summer vacation and leave the house to Keith. The way Keith, Nicole and Johnathan made it seem, I thought that there was going to be a lot of people there. I later found out that it was just going to be us four. Once again Johnathan used his soft tone and sweet words to try and get me to go to bed with him. I had a feeling that he was going to try something so I prepared myself for the face that he would put on that made me change my mind every time. I wasn't going to let him do it this time. His pitiful face wasn't going to get him anywhere this time. When I said "no," it seemed as if something awful just came over Johnathan. He began to get red in the face and I could tell that he was steamin' mad. I could also tell, by the smell on his breath that he had been drinking. Johnathan wouldn't take "no" for an answer. He beat me up and then raped me.

When we left Keith's house I didn't want to call the police because, like a dummy, I kept telling myself that I still loved him and that he only did it because he wanted to show me how much he loved me. Although I kept lying to myself I still felt nasty, naked, ashamed and embarrassed. When I got home I ran the hottest water I could stand and sat in the tub. I guess I felt like sterilizing myself, cleansing myself of the things I had just done. While sitting in the tub I started crying because I knew that I had to tell my parents and when I did it was going to hurt them very badly.

When my parents arrived home I sat them down at the table and told them everything. I had never seen my father cry before but I did that day. My heart just fell apart when I saw my father crying, my mother was in a state of shock. She just sat there. Tears were running down her face but she didn't move or say a word. I was worried about her.

Two weeks had passed and I hadn't heard from my dear Johnathan. I wasn't sure what was wrong so I decided to call him. When I called he treated me like a stranger, like one of his enemies. I asked him why was he treating me so badly and he said that I was acting like a baby and that he didn't want to go with a baby. He dumped me right then and there. I must have cried for about three hours straight. My mother, father, Nicole, and even the school counselors tried to give me comforting words to help me get through the pain of what I had done and the pain of losing Johnathan. It seemed as though no one knew the right words to say. I was just hoping that it would all go away. No matter how much I tried to forget everything, my thoughts, memories, and dreams seemed to always haunt me. I just wished that I could start all over.

BEAUTY IS IN
THE EYE OF VIRTUE

In this next section I'm going to talk about a situation that has been going on for a long time and is still going on today. In no way am I trying to make myself seem like I'm better than anyone else.

There is an old saying that, "beauty is in the eye of the beholder." At times we as kids, and some adults, tend to down talk other people because of their looks, style, or even their culture. When we do this we're only making it harder for those who already think that they are unattractive. We need to understand that everyone is beautiful in his or her own way. My sister tells me, everyone knows someone that thinks that they are ugly and someone that thinks they are pretty or handsome. Although some people may find that hard to believe, it's true.

To those who may think negatively about their looks, I want to tell you something that I think is important for you to know. Too often people wear tight, revealing or skimpy clothes because they don't feel pretty. Just like there is someone who may think you are ugly there is also someone who thinks you are pretty. Understand that the world doesn't revolve around our opinion of other people neither other's opinion about us.

When you talk about people and you don't think that you are doing any harm you could be wrong. What if a person heard your comments and your comments only added to what others have said about them? Sooner or later if the comments become too much to handle then something tragic could happen.

While some people wear tight clothes to fit in with the crowd, some people give up sex to fit in. They think that if they give up sex they will be a part of a special group. We need to let them know that if there is such a group then they don't want to be a part of it. We need to tell them that in the end the only thing that will matter is their self-respect and their purity. It is what's on the inside that really counts. When many are dead because of AIDS those who did not follow the crowd will realize the mistake they could have made. I want to tell anyone that this applies to that there are plenty of groups that don't care about your style, your color or your sexual life. That's the kind of group that you need to be in.

LOOK AT WHAT'S NEXT

Allow me to introduce some pretty important people in my life. Each of them has some very special advice to share with us based on their life experiences.

The first word of advice comes from my very own grandmother. We call her Granny. She is so wise and when she speaks, I listen.

The second writer is my mother. My mom is a woman of wisdom and I just don't know a smarter woman. She really gives me someone to look up to. Because she is ambitious, I have now become ambitious. We laugh together and have great fun.

Last, but certainly not least, is my dad. Daddy is what you may call an "involved father." Everything that concerns me concerns him. I think that because he is a pastor and he counsels a lot of people he is more in tune with the real issues of today's society. He also serves to help motivate me to write and be creative.

After Granny, Mama, and Daddy finish with their part I have a lot of good friends who have been interested in this book since I started. Since they were so interested I thought it might be cool to let them say something that can be meaningful to us all.

As we said in the beginning of this book the names of the characters have been change in some instances. This is for the protection and privacy of those indicated. Don't let anybody fool you, each story is real.

I hope that you will enjoy these writings from my family and friends as much as I have.

YOU TELL 'EM GRANNY

Chrissy, Grandma is so proud of you. Now don't you go tryin' to correct my grammar cause I ain't got that much time left on earth to go to school. You are such a pretty girl. You've got a lot of your mamma's ways in you. Of course you look like your daddy a little, but you are the spitting image of your mom. If you can follow her example you will be alright 'cause she is a good girl.

Baby, Grandma haven't even finished all the way your first book and here you are writing another one. This one is going to be good too. Cause we all need to be more, you know, that *virgin* word.

Things are a heap different from the way they used to be. Back when I was a girl we weren't doing all of this stuff they are doing now. If somebody got "messed up" (pregnant) then the family would hide it. In some cases I'm sure they fixed the problem (abortion) and the next time that you seen the girl she was looking like herself again. We were not allowed to go around anyone who had broken her leg (this was the way the older people described being pregnant.) You would hear them say, "You know, Mary don' gon' and broke her leg." They would seldom use words like *pregnant*. "She put a cast on it" meant that the girl would keep her baby. "She will be up and about in a minute," meant abortion. It wasn't every day that you would hear about this kind of stuff. A heap of us took pride in being pure and saving ourselves until we got married, or at least let me say, I did.

Baby your granddaddy was a handsome man with big eyes and fair skin, and oh, could he dress neat. I really wasn't studin' him. He would smile at me and try to hold my hand but I would not let him. Then one day he asked my daddy for my hand in marriage and daddy said, "yes." That's how we got married. He knew I was a virgin and he was proud of it. We would have been married 57 years if he were still living. Of course you know he died in 1984.

I don't know if you remember your granddaddy or not. He always told me that a man wanted a good woman. That's what I tried to be. I ain't known but one man in all my life and I don't want to know another one. Your granddaddy was enough for me. I don't know how some people can do the things that they do, run around with every Tom, Dick and Harry. Not me, and I had better not catch you doing it. You stay pure and keep yourself for your husband.

There are all kinds of things that can happen to you now, seases (diseases), viruses and other stuff that I cannot even say. Of course ya'll always pick at me about the way I talk anyway, specially your sister, Precious. How is she? She was liking a boy one time wasn't she? I told her to be careful and you too, and keep your dress tail down. Make good use of that word "no" and I mean *NO!*

I was your age when Daddy and Momma seen that your granddaddy, Odie, was flirting with me. They let him come to the house to see me, course we couldn't court yet. They kept the door opened and blinds pulled up. He would have to tell his mother when he was coming to see me. She would tell him, "Make sure you behave because that's a mighty good girl over there and Bob Freeman (your great-granddaddy) will kill you if you mess with her." He knew it too. He was a perfect gentleman. However whenever Daddy would turn his back or go to feed the mule and the cow, Odie would try to get mannish, but I would give him the big *NO!* He did not want daddy to hear me saying *no*. When I said it I really meant it. I want you all to mean it too.

Your granddaddy would make me feel so good; telling me how proud he was that I was a virgin. I can't say this word too loud. Back then we didn't say it at all. When you get married I want you to remember that the white dress you wear means something and don't you forget it. You will wear it so pretty. You may be young but you know right from wrong. Keep doing the right thing. You are a good example to follow.

Your mother, Donna, has always been a special girl. She was never like some of the other girls when she was coming up.

When your daddy picked her I knew she was good, but I was still concerned about him. Of course he came out alright. You have good parents. Listen to them and obey them. I was always so scared to not obey my parents. I just knew that God would get me if I disobeyed. Because of this I was kept and married as a virgin. I'm proud that I have only had one man in my life.

Men were always saying something to me but I didn't pay them any attention. They didn't mean me no good, just wanted to mess up my name. They didn't and don't you let them have your name. Listen to your daddy, he knows you may think that he is hard on you sometimes but it is because he loves you very much. Make sure you teach your brother, *Spēciál* how to be a gentleman. Ain't he a mess? If he grows up to be like his daddy he will be alright.

You ain't trying to date are you? I hope not. You are still a little young. If you are, go with a crowd, stay out of the dark and practice the word, *no*. If he does not like you for saying *no* then get rid of that boy, cause he doesn't mean you any good. A man ought to appreciate a girl who will say *no*. The buzzards come to spoiled meat so keep yourself pure and clean, just like you are.

Grandmamma don't have much more to say. I'm almost eighty years old and I can't think like I used to, but I can see a no good boy. So, make sure that I meet him and listen to my grunts and watch my side-view looks. That will tell you how I feel about him.

You are going to be alright, I just know it. I can see it in your smile. Your personality is so much like your mother. I'm proud of all my grandchildren. I've got so many. When I see my Lord I will be glad to hear Him say, "Eunice well done, only one man and an example for many.

Grandma's got to go now and have a cup of coffee. You stay sweet and give everyone my love.

Grandma Eunice

A MOTHER'S INPUT

In today's times, virtue and chastity are almost unheard of. As a matter of fact they are rarely thought of, even among us as parents. Where are the days of instilling into our children a sense of respect for their bodies and respect for others? I am grateful that respect for others was instilled in me during my childhood. It has gotten me where I am today.

I have no regrets for being different in my younger years. At fifteen years of age I was surrounded by teens that wanted to experience the adult scene earlier than they should. Unfortunately, they later paid for their choices. During my teen years I recognized that the word *virgin* was not a dirty word. Within my commitment to virginity I found myself feeling like the misfit, outcast, weirdo and oddball because I chose not to follow the crowd. Early in my life I decided to take a stand and not conform to the crowd. I remember making a pact with my best friend that we would not have sex until we were married and that we would stay pure. I kept my part of the deal; I am not sure what she did.

I was a normal teen. I enjoyed music, movies, and love stories with happy endings. These are the very same things that normal kids like today, I think. Mostly I wanted to know that anything I did in my present would not haunt me in my future. Maybe I was somewhat mature for my age but this is just the way I thought.

A great author once wrote that "youth is a continual intoxication" and I totally agree. Many times, immature thinking can cloud ones' decision making. When I think about my younger days there was a great influence to drink, smoke and have sex. Even as young as elementary school age, yes I said elementary, those influences were there. I don't remember judging my peers for what they chose to do but I just knew it was not for me.

As far as I can remember, the promise I made with my best friend was not discussed after that. However, deep down I felt it necessary to keep that promise. I have found that the best way to keep a promise is to be serious and focused. I never walked around trying to be different in my outward appearance ("holier than thou") but it always seemed that my promise and firm decision was a personal commitment. When guys were around, I was very particular about how I carried myself. I made sure that what we talked about was clean. My biggest conviction was God being pleased with whatever I did or said.

Young people are precious and they should feel that all that belongs to them (the body) is precious. They should cherish their bodies and demand that they are not treated as an item to lie down and to be used up. They should be appreciated and that appreciation should last longer than the short moment in which they are told, "I love you."

To know that I have only been with one man in my life, even to this day, makes me feel special. If he never knew that he was the only man, I would still feel special. Yes, sometimes I have wondered if I missed out on anything by being so adamant about chastity. But when I hear my husband speak highly of my morality I can appreciate the pride that he expresses when he speaks of me. I also have an inner joy when I talk to my daughters and their friends. Although they feel the pressure of being different, I can encourage them to hold on. When teaching them my focus is not past situations but taking a stand from the point of discovery that you are special. I encourage them to keep a clean life for God and the man that they will marry.

Virginity is not a lost art; it is a virtue that has been overlooked as important. We must return to the true values of life and recognize that as we live we must set examples for our children. Allowing our children to indulge in anything that can raise their curiosity level to that of adult activity is wrong; this can include smoking, drinking, having sex, etc. Parents have the responsibility of teaching their children values such as virginity.

Sometimes our children think that we don't understand them. I have never forgotten what it is like to be young. I remember this guy, who was supposed to be my boyfriend, boldly asking me to have a baby for him. We had not even talked about having or indulging in sex. I found it very STUPID and FOOLISH for him to assume that I would do something like that. There was no mention of love or that he cared enough to even want to marry me. I believe it was just a contest he was in with his friends to see who could prove their manliness first, by getting a girl pregnant. I was not the one! That same boy came back to me months later and whispered, "Since you would not give me a baby I found someone who did." As I looked in the direction in which he was pointing I saw his new girlfriend and yes, she was obviously pregnant. I felt sorry for her.

That situation occurred over 25 years ago. While times have changed, it appears that the way young men think has not changed very much. The mindset of getting a girl pregnant to prove manhood is very much alive today. Our young girls are failing to realize that they have a greater price to pay in the act of sex than the young man. They must consider that pregnancy and possibly infections cause wear and tear on their bodies. There are mental battles that the girl's future companion may have. Chrissy, don't ever allow your standards to be jeopardized or be in competition with your male friend's virtues or standards. For reasons unknown there appears to be a difference between women and men's acceptance of standards.

When I was in high school, ninth grade as a matter fact, I had a crush on an older high school athlete. He was so cute. I became stupefied (*to make stupid, groggy, or insensible*) whenever he came around but I never wondered about or considered sex. I just thought he was "tops." This athlete was not my only infatuation during that time. I was also infatuated with a professional singer and various movie stars. Sometimes my crushes were so strong I thought it was love. I'm saying these things to let young people know that these are very natural feelings and emotions but they do not have to lead you to think that sex is necessary.

There are outside forces that can create for you as an individual, an urgency to have sex, such as letting someone kiss you or touch you in your private areas, watching sexually explicit movies, reading books and magazines that have sexual orientations. Avoiding petting, fondling, touching and kissing can help to guarantee you that you will not compromise your commitment to remain a virgin because it takes more than a crush to have sex. Once you come to find out what it feels like to have someone caress you, you will naturally start to desire more than that. An intimate hug or kiss from a non-relative can have a greater impact than a warm hug or kiss from a dad, mom or siblings. What I felt for that athlete, actor, and singer was just a crush and no more than that. To have a crush or to be infatuated with someone is to have a strong like, or a foolish extravagant admiration, short of love.

Stay away from the crowd who supports the thinking that, "everyone is doing it." Don't trust guys who say, "It will be special and I won't treat you differently." Dear ones just remember that what has been placed in your possession is for you to protect and cherish. Keep it from contamination and danger and make that possession last as long as you can. Your body, virtue and virginity are possessions. Always feel that they are possessions, special treasures preserved for a special person and a special time.

Now that I am an adult, I reflect back that my concern and desire to remain chaste sometimes felt strange. I often wondered if something was wrong with me because I felt different and few to none spoke about virginity in a positive way. I think that if peers got together (especially guys) and took a stand to beat the odds to stay a virgin, which really is not odd, and allow that stand to come to fruition (realization), we would decrease teen pregnancy, thus reducing feticide (abortions), STDs and the AIDS population.

Teens, it is important that you elevate your values and worth of life as well as the health of your body. It would put a freeze on our youth's low esteem and the suicide rates. Unwed teen pregnancies would decrease, which happens mostly because of a need to love and/or be loved. A sense of value and importance in one's self always raises the esteem level to the highest. As parents, we must continue to push and encourage our youth to be better. In doing this we will find that we will have a safer society to live in and we can have outstanding future adults for our country to depend on to secure our future.

There are two major reasons that made me stick to the promise I made to myself. The first is that I was confident in knowing that what I wanted in life would make me happy and the second was I didn't allow anyone to put pressure on me to change. I wanted to be happy knowing that I had made the right choice.

The day I married was a very important day for me. I knew I would be married to only one man for the rest of my life and that I would not commit adultery. It has happened. I have only had one man. Was it hard to do? No, not at all. I always knew that I should not have sex until marriage. I also knew that I should love the man that I married. Any compromise was forbidden. The community knew it, my peers knew it and most of all I knew it. Throughout my adult life, other people seemed to be excited about my virginity and being intimate with only one man. I never saw it as a big issue because I knew what I wanted from the beginning. My husband picks and jokes with me about being a virgin when we married. However, he always ends the conversation with, "I'm glad that you were."

When I was dating my husband, he wanted to marry me after my high school graduation. I declined because finishing college was too important. I'm sure that I would not have gained a career if I had married at that time. I would probably have gotten pregnant and school would have been put on the back burner.

In essence, I have no regrets from the past. If I had to do it again, I would do it the exact same way. Now it is my desire, as a parent, to encourage my children to grow up to be outstanding, upright God-fearing adults. I do not regret my past because I can give my children input for their lives by my example. The statistics regarding STDs and the AIDS population is frightening and it must stop somewhere. We may not be able to control these statistics from a large populous, but as individuals we must take a stand and not contribute to this epidemic, which has come because of a lack of self-control, poor esteem, no fear of God, and a desire to please oneself.

The best decision in my life, besides salvation, has afforded me the pleasure of writing this section in my daughter's book. To Chrissy and all who read my story, remember that what you do today will always be a memory. You will have good and bad situations but you can make the best of them all. Take a stand for what you believe in and be prepared to prove and defend it. Do not allow anyone, especially peers, to change your decisions. The price you must pay for the things you do in life can be permanent. Consult with others about life's choices, particularly those that have been through the same things (adults). Continue to have God in your life because ultimately He is the head of your life. Remember that ONLY WHAT YOU DO FOR GOD WILL LAST!

Mom

FATHER KNOWS BEST

I'm Chrissy's dad and as she says her "greatest motivator." It would probably be in order if I were to say how proud I am of her, however I think that should go without saying. Along with being proud of her I am very concerned. She's a young lady who is stepping out and talking about a very needed but shunned subject, being a virgin. Not only is she a virgin but she is advocating others to be also. It's frightening to know that there is much hidden pressure associated with being a virgin. The pressures are so strong that some who are virgins do not want to admit that they are. They whisper to those with whom they are willing to be honest and say, "Yes, I am a virgin but do not tell anyone."

Will someone please tell me what these pressures are? Are virgins afraid that they will be mocked or picked at? Isn't the pride of being a virgin greater than the mockery associated with being a virgin? Why are you shy, ashamed, embarrassed, and downright afraid for anyone to know that you are a virgin?

Men who were virgins when they married are almost afraid to let anyone know this. Why, is still my question? What will the world say to you about being a virgin? Will they say that you missed out and that you don't know what you are missing? If we add up the facts, and we should, to not be a virgin is to fornicate. To fornicate is to sin. Therefore the pressure is to sin. To be ashamed to admit that you have not sinned is to say quietly that you wished you had.

Where is this pressure coming from? It emanates from the kingdom of Satan. He would like for all, men and women to have AIDS, STDs and the burden of abortions; this would really please the enemy.

Need I remind you that you cannot immaculately conceive? You can only get pregnant or have abortions from being pregnant if you are having sex. I really wish that it were an honor to all of those who are virgins to share that they are. I believe this may remove some of the pressure upon those who are virgins but will not admit that they are because of the embarrassing image of being a virgin. There is absolutely nothing wrong with being a virgin. Having been with only one man or woman is a moral and chaste honor. There are many that wish that they had your testimony, one man or one woman.

Chrissy, you and all others who are virgins are very special people. Do not let the persuasive thought that you are a virgin only because you are young dissuade you from maintaining your virginity. Your mother has set a great example for you and before her your grandmother. It can be done, one man in your entire life. There are many people who have this testimony. Maybe now they will start writing and sharing their experiences and we can put it in the next print of *Happy On A Virgin's Island.*

Baby, when you start feeling pressured, talk to your mom. She is an amazing woman who will be there for you. The reason many yield to the pressure is because for some reason they cannot find someone to talk to. When I look at your mom and see her chastity and morality, I'm proud that God allowed me to marry a virgin. I do not intend to demean anyone else's marriage but neither do I intend to sell short the power of morality, chastity and virginity.

Please dream with me. Everyone is a virgin until marriage. STDs, abortions, etc. are at an all time low. Okay, wake up. Wouldn't that be absolutely wonderful?

I think that this pressure problem is because people do not understand that the expressed testimony of one being a virgin is a potent ministry for many others. Yes, I said ministry. There are those who will read this book and say "I won't, I don't; don't even try it. This book is going to save many people from future harm and emotional problems. Thank you Chrissy for opening up the door to so many young people who needed someone else to keep the virgin ball rolling.

Hopefully millions of copies of this book will circulate. If so then we would know that our goal has been met. We would have helped many to maintain and others to sustain themselves in chastity and celibacy. My prayer is that all virgins will have the boldness to say that they are virgins. The world is waiting to hear that it is being done.

Please remember these points: you can't take back your virginity once it is gone. Seldom will one marry the one they lose their virginity to. Virgins will never have to worry about getting pregnant and going through the emotional battle of having an abortion, AIDS and other diseases. These things will be kept far from you. Virginity is one of the greatest compliments to marriage. Keeping your name out of the guys' black books makes them egotistically mad. And finally most people ultimately respect a virgin. I love you and have enjoyed helping prepare this book.

Dad

IF I COULD TURN BACK THE HANDS OF TIME

Often things will happen in your life, things that you would like to have the opportunity to go back and change. Just remember, that "your past is the fertilizer for your future," (Pastor James S. Prothro) and you should learn and grow from it.

Being a virgin is great because everyone looks up to you and they sing the praises of your name. Coping with the pressures of being a virgin, as we grow older can be confusing because of the peer pressure, the mockery of disbelief and curiosity. Just as a word of warning, there are very few people who will believe you when you say that you are a virgin, probably because people are not very sensitive to truth. What I am really trying to say is I believe a very high percentage of the people who say that they believe you, walk away talking under their breath saying, "Yeah, that's what you want me to think." You must have confidence in the fact that you are a virgin. If no one else believes you that is not your problem. As I stated earlier, life can be confusing enough without involving other people's drama also. However, this confusion does not at all compare to the confusion that comes with losing your virginity. Believe me when I say, "It is not worth it to lose your values."

Crushes and infatuations are common and natural when you are young. I mean infatuations may come like the seasons in a year. They will pass if you just enjoy them but do not let them take you where you do not need to go. In other words, just have fun. There are movie stars, singers and even those around you on daily bases that are much older than you that attract your interest. Remember that although these crushes are natural still, if not controlled, they may not always be healthy. Too often they will stir up feelings and emotions that you really do not need to deal with. Allow me to share my story:

Around the age of nine or ten, I was beginning to become curious about sex. I had heard things from my friends, from movies and television, and even from my own inner thoughts based on my observations of life. What was this three-lettered word, S-E-X, all about? My friends spoke so highly of their sexual experiences; the television shows made sex seem so glamorous, yet the adults in my life warned me against it.

Let me advise Chrissy and all who are reading this book do not be afraid of your thoughts or curiosities. Find someone to talk to and they will tell you just what to do with them. They are normal and natural. Different people handle them in different ways.

When I was younger I would wonder when would I know what sex felt like and when could I join in on the fun? Little did I know this was not something that should be considered fun, not at a young age. When you are young you often look at things and desire them because you think that they will help you to grow up faster. You think that you can handle things that you see others do. I'm begging you to please be careful and stay young for as long as you can.

Playing house was the closest I had come to being physically involved with anyone and playing was all that I wanted. Now follow me closely as I show you just what I mean when I say that experienced curiosity is much more confusing than that of the inexperienced.

Coincidentally, as my curiosity about sex was growing, the opportunity to know firsthand presented itself sooner than I thought I was prepared. Be careful young ladies because what you desire is probably not at all what you really need. As the older generation says, "Be careful of what you ask for because you may just get it."

Secretly, I had had a crush on Jeffrey since the day that I first saw him. He was seven years older than I was and to me he was a hunk, so fine. I envied the women he hung out with and began trying to compete with them. Can you believe that little young me against grown mature them? I wanted to be wherever he was and to do whatever he did.

This became really easy for me to do because he had a sister, Lena, who was my age. Lena and I were good friends.

Jeffrey allowed us to hang out with him. This made me feel really, really good because it gave me the opportunity to be in his presence. I guess he knew I had this crush on him because often when he took us out he referred to me as his "little girlfriend." The "little" word did not matter much to me because I didn't really pay it any attention. All I heard was "girlfriend."

I have since learned to be careful of what guys tell you because they will often say exactly what they need to say to get you off the Virgin's Island. I now know that being a virgin is attractive to some men for ego reasons, just so they can say, " I was the one," as if we are nothing but a prize hunt.

"Wow," I thought, "he actually called me his girlfriend." Needless to say I wasn't even a teenager, only a "teeny bopper." Never did I hear anyone ask him any questions about my age. This was probably because I looked so mature for my age. I thought this mature look was a good thing. It often gave me to act a little older as well. Often young people try to impress others to think they are older than they are without realizing that this can get you in "old trouble" as well. Stay young as long as you can, there is plenty of time for the ache and pains of maturity.

It was not uncommon for Lena and I to hang out at each other's home. One day, while Lena, her sisters and I were lying on the floor talking and laughing, Jeffrey came into the room. He began laughing and playing along with us. We had loads of laughs. Finally we all went to sleep.

Over into the wee hours of the morning, a hand rubbing my posterior awakened me, and it did not feel like a mistake. I looked up and Jeffrey was kneeling over me looking for my reaction. Quickly I sat up. I was scared, curious, excited and nervous all at the same time. I did not respond, instead I laid back down and tried to get back to sleep. Twice after that, in the same night, it happened again.

When Lena woke the next morning, I told her what had happened. She convinced me that we should tell someone because that shouldn't have happened. I agreed and we told an adult friend of ours. When Jeffrey was confronted he denied it. I felt bad because I thought he would be mad at me for getting him in trouble. I thought he might never call me his "little girlfriend" anymore.

Never be scared to tell when you have been violated. You don't deserve that and you don't have to take it. Although these thoughts raced through my mind, I yet knew that telling someone was the right thing to do.

Days later, Jeffrey and I talked and it turned out that he was upset but it was because I actually thought he would violate me like that. He promised me that he would never do anything like that. (He was lying.) Well, after that came the bomb.

It was Sunday afternoon in the winter of 1988. Again I was at Lena's house. Jeffrey was home along with the rest of the crew. He came in Lena's room where we were and asked her to leave because he needed to speak with me about something. When she left the room, he closed and locked the door. I wondered what he was doing. In my mind I continued to hear the words he told me, "I would never do anything to hurt you." These soothing words made me relax a little and somewhat let loose and trust him. His motives were not hidden yet I tried to hide them behind his previously spoken words, "I am not going to hurt you." Boy was I wrong!

He laid down beside me and began holding my hands. I asked him what he was doing and he said, "Nothing I just want to talk." Often when young people begin to date they think they have control and power to abstain from whatever they do not want to do. Things begin by simply holding hands, i.e. at the movies. There is the warmth of sexuality, but they don't even know what they are feeling. Although this seems so innocent it is where it all begins. So young people be careful and keep your hands to yourselves and everyone else's hand off of you. Now, back to the story.

He started by touching and petting and he was moving so quickly. I became confused. "Why was he doing this? Why wouldn't he stop?" This was what half of me felt, while the other half of me yearned for him to continue. I said, "stop" over and over again. I was scared of what my parents would think.

What would my friends say? Well, he must have heard my thoughts because he said, "Make sure you don't tell anyone because this is just between you and me." Do not ever trust anyone who tells you it's between you and me when it's wrong. It's only a trap.

Let me speak to young girls first. Watch what you keep a secret. There should always be things that you keep to yourself, yet there are things that you should talk about and ask questions about. Your feelings, curiosities, etc. are the kinds of things you share with those who can help you. When things don't feel right and it feels that someone is coming into your personal aura that's when you should tell. Find someone you can talk to, even if you can't talk to your parents. I can't help but continuously mention that these are very confusing times, whether you realize it or not. I knew that what he was doing was not right. My body confused me, my mind confused me, who was I to turn to and was I to let this happen?

Now to the guys, you can also learn to say "no." These days, girls are a lot bolder and they try things a lot more freely. However, that doesn't mean that you have to do what others may suggest. You don't have to follow the crowd. You can be a virgin also. The "black book" game is old and girls such as Chrissy and her friends are learning the art to your game. The sexual encounters that you hear older guys brag about are lies most of the time. These lies get bigger and bigger. Tell the truth and just be you.

While we were in the room, he continuously told me that there was nothing to fear. He promised me that he would never hurt me and he would take his time and be gentle at what he was tricking me into doing. I believed him because I really wanted to believe him. By now I was sobbing and trying to yell for him to stop. (I say trying because he covered my mouth). All of a sudden he let out a roar that actually made me even more afraid and he then got off of me. This man must have a mental problem I thought. He looked strange. "What was that? Why was he making that noise? Is he hurting too? What was going on?" (Of course now I know what it all was.)

He had violated me and satisfied himself at the same time. I was no longer a virgin. Shouldn't I have been happy and feeling good? Well I wasn't. I was hurt emotionally, physically, mentally, psychologically, and most of all I was alone. I didn't know what to do because I didn't know what I felt.

He asked me if I was alright and had the nerve to say, " I love you." I could not respond, but with tears in my eyes, I turned toward the wall. Lena knocked on the door and inquired about what was going on. Jeffrey told her that we were almost finished talking and that we would be out soon. He told her to leave us alone.

I went to the bathroom and I just stared in the mirror. I felt nasty, I felt dirty, very unclean. I was hurting and desired not to ever do that again. I was trembling and really confused. I wondered, "What if I'm pregnant? I don't want to have a baby. What if I have a disease?" All of this went through my mind.

I later got up the nerve to ask him these questions. He told me not to worry about having a disease. I asked him if he had had a disease and he said no and that he had been with no one but me. He told me not to worry about being pregnant because I could not get pregnant on my first time. (He lied. You can.) How stupid does that sound? It does not take an expert to be pregnant neither to get a disease. Statistics show that the smallest hole in a condom is bigger than the smallest AIDS cell. Now how's that for protection? Now that I am older and have experienced a lot of things, I know that he was saying what he had to say to get me to do it again.

Well, later that evening, I had to go to church. It was an evening of Holy Communion. (This is where we commemorate the death, burial and resurrection of Jesus Christ.) As I walked down the aisle I thought I would die as soon as I touched the communion cup. Yes, I had asked God for forgiveness for "whatever" had happened. I say "whatever" because I was still unsure of just what had happened. I knew that it was wrong, but at the same time it felt a little okay. Wouldn't you know it, that night the minister spoke on self-condemnation and about God being a forgiving God. I knew all of this, but somehow it all sounded so foreign and new to me.

Not many days after my experience with Jeffrey, my menstrual cycle began. I couldn't help but notice how my body was really developing. My feelings about sexuality were growing and my curiosity had become many times greater. I found myself desiring to have sex more than ever, while at the same time hating what had already happened. I knew that my feelings were wrong, yet I could not get rid of them. My emotions were intensifying to the point that the words "my little girlfriend" felt so much stronger and meant so much more. To me, I was his girlfriend, the real deal.

He began writing me letters, and of course I was instructed to discard them after I read them. He said that he loved me and I really felt that he did. He paid for me to have my nails manicured, he paid for my beeper, he gave me money, and he was really my boyfriend. However, I'm sure you know nothing in life is free. Do not take money or gifts from any man.

Three years later I remained trapped by this relationship. My mind had been raped and there seemed to be no end to the drama. I was out of control and could not help myself. I needed to have told my parents. I believe that not saying anything was a big mistake. My parents loved me and could protect me. Each time after the first time became easier and easier and actually was a delight to me (so I thought).

One day, I had finally decided that I wanted it all to stop. I hid from Jeffrey and would not answer my phone. What was this I was feeling? Was it too late? Had I ruined my future? I wanted to be a virgin again. I cried, "Will someone please give me back my virginity? Please help me cope with the loss," was my prayer. Jeffrey would not stop in his efforts to ruin me by using me.

One day I was at Lena's house while she was at school (she got out of school for summer vacation a week after me). I was in bed, asleep. I heard a knock at the front door. I looked out the window and I saw Jeffrey's car. Jeffrey had moved out and was no longer living at home. I thought, "He must not have his key." I did not go to the door because I had decided, no more, I just wasn't going to do it anymore. After the knocking stopped, I was relieved. I got out of the bed and went to look out the door. Suddenly, I heard tapping on Lena's bedroom window. It was a two-story building with bushes at the first level, and Lena's family lived on the second level. So how had he climbed up to the window? When I looked out of the window, I realized that he had not climbed up but he was throwing rocks at the window, trying to get my attention. He was calling my name very softly. I hid in the corner, trying not to even breathe because I did not want him to know that I was there. Finally he left.

A little while later, the phone rang. I did not pick it up because I knew that it would be him. The phone rang about ten minutes later. I answered it because I didn't know if it was Lena's parents calling or perhaps my own parents. It was Jeffrey. Our conversation went like this:

Me: "Hello," I said trying to sound sleepy.
Jeffrey: "Why wouldn't you answer the door? I know you heard me knocking."
Me: "I didn't hear you, I was asleep when the phone rang." (I lied.)
Jeffrey: "Well I'm coming back, so open the door."

He did just as he said and I had no choice but to open the door. I kept thinking to myself not today, I really don't feel like this today. This one thought just kept racing through my head.

When he came in we watched television for a brief while. The soap operas were on. He told me how we would someday be like some of those couples on the stories, just as soon as I turned 18. He promised that he would one day stand up to my dad and tell him that he loved me and then we could really be together. Girls, please watch those empty promises, they don't amount to anything.

84

His words made me feel good and once again he had me where he wanted me, ready to have sex. That's all that those words meant. They were just words to butter me up. Size up the words and see if they really make sense. Don't allow guys to treat you as if you are stupid, because that's what some aim to do.

By this time things had been going on for a while. There was not much enjoyment, just sex. No real feeling, no real desire, nothing to really look forward to. Actually it hurt, both mentally and physically and I wanted him to stop. I wanted to tell someone, I needed some help. I was told, "If you love me, you'll keep this to yourself." My friends knew, yet they covered by never saying a word.

Don't trust everyone that says they are your friends. Sometimes they are really out to bring you down. They come around just to learn about your weaknesses and the downfalls in your life. You must learn what to tell and what to keep to yourself. I now continue to remember that jealousy has many, many faces and none of them love you. Some of my friends couldn't help me because they were jealous of me.

I could not tell anyone how I felt neither could I talk to anyone. I felt that if I said something the adults in my life would be mad and would stop me from seeing him. Was that altogether a bad thing though? I really didn't know. Yes, I wanted him to stop and at the same time I wanted him never to leave me alone. My peers raved about me being with "an older man" and they did what we all thought was cute, "looked up to me." Little did we know.

Find some one to look up to that does something positive with his/her life, someone that feels that they are someone without the assistance of anyone else. Find a true mentor. I know a really good mentor, Crystaline Prothro, a young, strong, positive, young lady.

Years later I still couldn't seem to pull away from Jeffrey. I began showing interest in other boys. I was still very confused because I often longed and desired to have sex although it made me feel bad. Sex, what was this really all about?

One day I decided that I would just break off the relationship. I liked other people and I could be with them if I desired. Again Jeffrey must have been reading my mind because he began saying things like I was his, my body belonged to him and if I gave it away to anyone else he would be mad at me. He told me that he loved me and soon we would be together. He told me that I needed to keep it a secret just a little while longer and if I really loved him I would. Well, I did love him so I thought I would just keep it a secret just a little while longer.

I don't know what I was thinking. You see two years prior to this he began living with a woman. He promised me that she was just a roommate. Though very smart and mature for my age, often questioning why things were the way they were; something still made me believe him.

One day I received some bad news; the "roommate" was pregnant with his baby. He promised me that it was just a mistake and that he did not really love her. He said it would not happen again and wouldn't you know it, two years later, she was pregnant again. With this new information came more empty promises.

That was it, the last straw. How long would I be so stupid? Don't ever let anyone hurt you over and over again. Just remember the old saying, "you slap me once, shame on you, slap me twice, shame on me." Always watch out for yourself and be sure that you're careful with you.

The day finally came when I told my father what had been happening. Of course, he was upset, hurt, shocked and experiencing whatever other feelings come with hearing this type of news. He was upset at me for not telling and upset with Jeffrey for what he had done. Worst of all, he was upset with himself for not seeing it (parents don't like to know their babies are hurting, were once hurting and they can't or couldn't help). After the initial shock from all the news he had received, Dad and I talked and boy was he a big help. From the day I told him even until today he has walked me through my healing process and has become the one man I know really cares about how I feel. My dad is one man I know who will never break his promises to me and the one man I really know loves me.

My parents could not be there for me neither could they help me out of the situation because they did not know. Girls, talk with your dads and let them teach you how boys think. Sometimes, we as youngsters, feel that our parents won't or don't understand, but they do. Believe me they do. Although, they fuss at times, it definitely is because they love us. Our parents are not our enemies they want us to talk to them and let them know what we are feeling. Talk about how you feel, ask questions about why you feel what you feel, and find out all you need to know by listening before experiencing.

It has been seven years and though I haven't seen Jeffrey in over five years, he yet lives with me. Though not physically, he lives in my thoughts, in my heart and as a part of my past. Let me say also he's in jail right now for drugs and drug related crime. I look back and I wish I could turn back the hands of time. I thank God that through it all He has kept me and I am able to share this experience with you.

When I look at Chrissy and her peers, I know why people sing the praises of a virgin. Fairer skin, younger bodies and vibrant minds clear from all kinds of mess. I have joined in with those that look upon them and now I want to say to them as others once said to me, "Keep your virginity until you are married." This applies to both boys and girls.

Now that this situation is over I would like to share a few lines of poetry as an expression of my freedom:

After this experience I am free
And I do what pleases me.
Not because of a threat from a man
Or because my mouth is covered by a hand.
It's because I have chosen to live my life
And because I was delivered by Jesus' stripes.
If you want to stay really happy and enjoy your life to the fullest that you can,
Stay on the Virgin's Island.

PEER PRESSURE TO PROVE

I am a young man with a problem. I feel pressure to have sex. I don't know why I feel this pressure or how to overcome it. I know very little about the consequences. Many of my friends are saying that they are having sex but I am not, so I feel cheated and behind the times. I'm not sure if they are being honest. I only know that I can't tell them that I am a *virgin*. What would they think of me?

I am a sports star. I have brilliant grades yet I have been lying to my friends about sex. I never meant to lie. It just came out. We were in a conversation about girlfriends and who was or was not a chump. We started telling our sex stories. The stories started getting bigger and bigger. Every boy was competing with the other for who had the most experience. I knew within myself that I was lying but I was not about to admit it. My interest in sex increased due to my lying. My thought was that this experience would be the fulfillment of my manhood.

I had had a few, and I mean a few, occasions where I got pretty close. It was nothing serious and to be honest I had not even kissed a girl. I picked out certain girls that I thought would be "easy" and even they were not willing to assist me in my endeavor to achieve manhood. At night I thought about having this experience and then I saw myself lying about already having experienced it. Sometimes I thought that I was being punished for lying and that's why I hadn't had sex yet. That's how confusing my life was.

From time to time I thought about the unwelcomed possibility of getting a girl pregnant. I knew that using protection would eliminate that though. What if she was experienced? I didn't know how to use protection and I felt like she would be able to figure that out. To fix that problem I began reading about it in books. I went to a store and stole a condom and practiced using it so that I would know how to use it, then I would not be embarrassed in front of my partner. The problem was I did not have a partner. I had several so-called girlfriends but most of them were not active or thinking about being active. I was not allowed to hang around the girls that hung out in the streets, which was another pressuring problem that I had. I didn't know how to fix my problem. I was the leader among my buddies. I admit that when I was around my buddies I perpetrated as though I was some sex education trainer.

I kept feeling that it was wrong to feel what I was feeling but my feelings were too strong to dismiss. My body was in trouble and my nature out of control. One day I decided to talk to an older friend, Eugene, who really helped me. He told me that what I was feeling was normal. That did not comfort me but when he told me that my friends were probably lying about having sex, I started feeling better. They too were lying? I was not the only one? I then realized that there were no girls admitting to our so-called experiences. No one had proven our stories. The pressure to fulfill our manhood had trapped us all.

The next time that I got with my buddies and we began talking on our usual subject of, "men having sex" I had a different attitude. No longer was I feeling like a fake. I felt that we were all alike, feeling pressured to have sex but not mentally ready to deal with the consequences. This feeling had come from television, magazines, etc. and most of all from nature itself. We were feeling what teenagers were supposed to feel. The course of nature was in process and we didn't know it.

We thought, or at least I did, that we should violate girls to prove our manhood. I know better now. I learned this lesson when I met this very nice girl who expressed that she only wanted to "go with" a virgin guy. Even to her I could not admit the truth. Before I knew it, I had protected the fact that I was a virgin by saying, "It's going to be hard to find a guy who is a virgin." She replied, "Well I'm going to keep looking until I do." She was not going out with any guy who was not a virgin.

Was I going to finally admit this thing or would I keep lying about it? Was it more important to perpetrate or to "go with" this beautiful girl? I had a decision to make. I cleared my throat and dropped my head and said in a low voice, "I am a virgin." She replied, "What did you say?" Embarrassingly I said it louder, "I am a virgin." She fell on her knees and held her stomach and would not stop laughing. Then I heard it for myself. "I told my friends you were a virgin and I didn't care what others said. There was something special about you that didn't fit the mold of being sexually active." At that moment I realized that she had tricked me. She had gotten me to confess that I was a virgin, as a part of a game. I asked her what was it about me that made her think I was a virgin? She never told me what it was but I knew it must have been something.

If it was that obvious did everyone know? Why hadn't someone told me that they knew? I was looking to blame some-one for my dishonest trap. As you may guess, the word got out. I was a publicly announced virgin but to my surprise, very few people mocked me. It wasn't as bad as I thought that it would be. I felt ashamed but not pressured. I found out that some of the other "renowned sex professors" had been lying also. The pressure from peers was so heavy and it had almost trapped me for life. I do know that it is okay to feel nature but it is not okay to experience it just because you feel it.

While sex is what we all may be curious about, our cu-riosity needs to be put on hold. The greater image is to be hon-est and not have sex. I want to say to all of my other teenage friends, what my pastor said recently in one of his sermons, "Don't lie about it and then you will not have to lie in the pain of life." I think he means be honest and honest then you will be. I hope that you are okay and have been helped by my story.

Anonymous 15 year-old male.

P.S. They really were lying

91

IT WASN'T WORTH IT

It wasn't long ago that I made a huge mistake. I didn't realize it then but I know it now. I was in love, so I thought, with one of the cutest, most popular guys in my school, Marcus. We had a pretty cool relationship. We talked on the phone a lot, he would walk me to and from class and he would walk me home after school. He was so sweet. As in many high school relationships, sooner or later, the topic of *sex* came up. The first few times I blew it off. I never actually thought we would do it.

As the topic continued to come up, I started wondering about a few things. I thought, "What if we did have sex? Would he break up with me or would he want to stay with me?" When I asked him these questions of course he said that he loved me and he wouldn't do that to me. He knew that I had never had sex before but it wouldn't be his first time. I told him I wasn't sure so he didn't bring up the subject for a while.

Then, it came up again, the big question. He said to me, "So when are you going to let me prove my love to you?" This time I seriously thought if I ignored his question would that mean that it was over between the two of us? I thought, "Well he says he loves me. He says he wouldn't leave me." I thought I loved him. Why shouldn't we have sex? We must be meant for each other. All kinds of thoughts kept running through my head. He told me he had never had a girlfriend like me and I would be the one that he would marry. When we were around each other I got butterflies in my stomach. He gave me this queasy feeling. I thought, "We've got to be in love."

Well, the day came that I chose to have sex with Marcus. I knew that I shouldn't have sex before marriage, but I went against what I knew. It was like I forgot everything I had been taught in that moment. My emotions and hormones just took over. I wasn't even thinking clearly. I didn't think about the fact that I could get pregnant or contract some kind of disease.

Well, we did it and when it was finally over I kept thinking what an unpleasant experience it was. It was terrible. It hurt and to tell you the truth, I didn't feel anything special. There were no feelings of love like I thought it would be. I felt very uncomfortable. What if I had waited and given it more thought? I definitely would not have had sex. I didn't realize that my virginity was one of the most precious things I had and I had just given it away like it was nothing. I gave it to someone who was not promised to always be in my life. Why did I feel as though I would spend my life with him? I didn't know for sure but I made a decision that I couldn't take back.

I had no idea what love was all about. I now know that love isn't just being physically attracted to someone or having a strong crush. A lot of people confuse affection with love. They think having sex is love. Some also have sex because they feel that their partner will not stay around if they don't. If that person really loves you then they will be there even if you don't have sex. There is a lot more to love than that.

When I decided to have sex with Marcus I put my whole future in jeopardy. Getting pregnant would have only gotten in the way of my future plans to go to college and be successful. Having a sexually transmitted disease could kill me. Most people would say, "You can use protection." Well, condoms don't always work.

Sex did nothing for our so-called relationship but make it more stressful. I already had school to worry about. Now this! I look back on the relationship and realize that it wasn't a partnership unless sex was involved. We didn't break up afterwards probably because he knew that if we had sex once then we would probably have sex again. I regret the decision I made but for a while I didn't realize that I could start over. You can become a virgin again.

Time went by and we ended up breaking up. I truly wish I had waited. Your first time is supposed to be special. That's why I truly feel that you shouldn't have sex until you get married. Your first time should be something to remember. I'm sure that most people wouldn't want to look back and say, "I actually lost my virginity to that person." Your virginity is meant to be a special gift you give to your husband or wife. If a person had to choose between something new and pure and something used up, don't you think they would choose something new?

I'm not trying to sound like a lecturer but abstinence is really the best decision to make. If you are in a relationship, abstaining from sex will keep your focus on building the relationship. Temptation will come but a very important thing is to have God in your life. You must trust in God. Ask God to guide you in everything you do from your thoughts to your actions. Overcome temptations by watching the environments you chose to be in. Watch the people you hang around. You are what you eat. If you continually feed yourself with unclean things then that's what you'll be, unclean. If you involve yourself in situations, movies, songs, etc. that talk about sex then that's what you'll want to do. Do the things that are pleasing to God. Temptations are very hard to overcome without Him.

REGRETTABLE

Hi, my name is Regrettable, I am nearly 30 years old now and I feel that I must share my story with you in hopes that I can help others, maybe you, to realize that what's important to you may not be important to someone else. I apologize wholeheartedly if the content of my story seems to be sexually explicit. While I do intend to keep it real, under no circumstances does Crystaline Prothro, Robot Publishing, or myself intend to endorse, suggest, or advocate sex before marriage. I certainly hope that my mistake can be used as knowledge for you therefore keeping you from making the same mistake. May God bless you as you read this story:

I grew up in a household where sex, profanity, etc. was not hidden from me. All I had to go on was Mama's phrase, "If you make your bed hard, you will have to lie in it."

At the age of 8 or 9 I started having sexual orientations. (I know that this is what it was now that I am an adult looking in hindsight.) These sexual curiosities became part of my everyday thoughts and conversation. This was not good. One of my friends told me that she was experienced and that she had been molested. She would always tell me that sex was okay. Now that I think about it, I think this was based on the fact that it happened to her and she was not bothered by it. There is a thin line between what is normal and natural and what is motivated by sexual curiosity.

As I grew older I became more and more confused because I began experiencing emotions as well as physical desires that I did not understand. I did not realize that this was a stage that I was going through. I was actually having sexual thoughts. I did know that sex was wrong and I did not want to have sex, but what were these feelings?

My body matured quickly. At the age of 11 the boy next door and I were good friends. There was one problem, he would always try to lure me into dark hidden places. He was two years older than me. At times when he would try his luring tactics I was reluctant yet desirous to go with him. I began feeling this strange sensation when I was around him, but I never allowed him to touch me. Again I say, thank God, I never let him touch me.

By the time I reached high school the real war began. I started wondering how it would feel to experience physical contact with a man. My spiritual and moral convictions would always interrupt my desires. Nevertheless I was having strong feelings about this.

During my 8th grade year I had friends who would talk about sexual acts that they engaged in. Some were allowed by their parents, so they said. They would express that their parent's sentiments were that they would rather give them birth control pills, condoms and a place to entertain their guest, than to have them going to sleazy hotels, picking up diseases, getting pregnant, etc. In my opinion, these should not be a parent's sentiments. I really didn't need to hear this kind of conversation because I was having sexual feelings about boys who I liked. I wanted to satisfy my curiosities but I reminded myself of Mama's words and became too afraid to do anything. (Thank God for wisdom.)

For the next few years of my life I experienced much peer pressure to become sexually active but I had a stronger determination to be celibate. No one knew and seemed to care that all this was happening to me, especially those that I really needed, my parents. To my close friends I was a "Miss Goody two shoes", a square.

I made it through high school and successfully held to my standard despite all the temptations. I seemed to be on my way. I went to college and was doing good, dating in groups or dating "safe guys." Things were in control until I turned 18. I began having even stronger sexual feelings. I had more knowledge about sex. In conversations with friends, both male and female, I was told about many sexual experiences, which sometimes included very graphic details. I did not realize that listening to the stories could trap me into the world of sex. My curiosities were stronger than ever.

I can't say that I was fully aware of what was going on when a male friend of mine had suddenly become the subject of my infatuation. He was extremely handsome, sexy, kind to me, and most of all he made me feel good about myself. When he complimented me I took them to be real. His compliments never seemed like lies that he was throwing out just to try to get me to have sex with him. He said things that made me feel good through and through. He never made any advances toward me and I respected him highly for that.

I remember calling him one day, after having dreamed about him, and I expressed to him my infatuations. He responded as though he understood my infatuations but did not want to take advantage of me. These infatuations grew, creating some difficult times for me over the next couple of years.

I thought about this man constantly. Sometimes I shared my thoughts. At the age of 20 I really desired to have sex but I had this standard and respect for the fact that I was still a virgin. I knew I had power that few seemed to possess, I was holding out. My friend who I was infatuated with never got out of place with me and when I was around him I was too afraid to make any advances toward him.

One day it finally happened. We were having a conversation. Within myself I was longing for him to hold me as he had in my dreams. I wanted to feel what I dreamed about. I often wondered if dreaming was wrong. I wanted him to have sex with me. I had never felt this kind of attraction before in my life; it was so strong. I did not tell him what I was feeling, but he knew.

He asked me if I was okay. I responded, "Yes," but, in my mind I was responding, "No I'm not. I'm about to lose my virginity. Do you think I can be okay?" Inside I was full of fear. Outside I appeared calm and I thought ready.

As I began to relax with him, he was so kind and warm, I felt so secure. I began thinking about so many different things that I had fantasized about, things, which for a moment caused me to lose all sense of rationale. When I realized what was taking place it was too late, I had done the most regrettable thing of my life. I had given up my virginity.

Immediately I began feeling regret and pain. My pain was both physical and emotional. He asked me if I was okay. He seemed to be very concerned and I could sense the genuineness of his concern. He asked me to hug him. After making sure I was okay he left.

Isn't that the way it always happens? You lose your most precious possession and he leaves to find another? I listened as his car started and he pulled off.

After I was sure he was gone, I fell to my knees. I was hurt physically, mentally and emotionally. I was angry and even more afraid than ever before. I knelt quietly crying. After a long bitter cry, I began crying out to God. You see, I was already professing salvation, and now I was feeling that I had disappointed my Lord and Savior. I was so confused and it was not worth it, not at all. We were both saved yet we had sinned. I began asking God to please forgive me because I felt so guilty. I asked Him to wash me and cleanse me because I felt so dirty. I asked Him to help me because I was so ashamed. After praying for myself I began praying for my friend. I asked God to have mercy on him, to cleanse him and to keep him.

After a long cry and a respectful prayer, I got up and went to the bathroom. I sat there almost in a daze. I was feeling as though I had given away something very precious. I had lost something, my virginity. I wanted to turn back the hands of time. I had done what I had fought against for many years. I had given away a very important part of me. The fact that I was an adult did not ease the pain. This was supposed to be a special thing for my husband and I to enjoy whenever I got married. Too late, I was soiled.

I did not become "wild" but after that experience, my desires became more of a struggle for me than ever before. I struggled after this, longing and fantasizing about that first time. It was painful and very emotional for me. It had not been the special time I thought it would be. I will forever remember that regrettable day when I lost my virginity. I'm so sorry that I did, I wish that I had never lowered my standards.

To Chrissy and all others, please cherish your virginity. It is more precious than anything. Through the peer pressure, the emotional merry-go-round, the confusion and everything else, you can make it. These seasons come and go. You know, if you are mature enough to read this book, you are mature enough to have had times when your natural desires were at high levels then suddenly things calmed down. You didn't care to even see the opposite sex. Your virginity is like a precious piece of jewelry. It is yours and when you lose it, it is not something that you can find again. The emotions that you experience are far worse than losing something materially valuable. Stay strong and wait on marriage. Giving away your virginity before marriage can be the most regrettable experience of your life. God will keep you and know that the only true friend is Jesus.

DON'T PLAY WITH FIRE, IT BURNS

Hello and welcome to my scenario. Part of my story took place in the West Indies and later in the United States. Being or not being a virgin is not an American thing; it is a pleasure or a problem all over the world. I am so excited that Chrissy has written this book and that she has chosen to include my scenario:

It was fall, 1983 and I was 21 years old. I had recently transferred to a university away from home. The pressures of remaining a virgin were beginning to build because I had reached the age that would qualify me as being grown. A few months prior to entering the university I was having mixed emotions regarding my sexuality. There were many things I wanted to do in life but I had not yet done them. Inclusive in those things that I did not need to do was having sex. In my household sex was not a subject we would discuss. Maybe it should have been discussed then I would have understood more clearly how normal it was to have sexual urges and not jeopardize my life and future by fulfilling that desire. In actuality I felt so alone.

I had been confronted several times by guys who selfishly desired to fill the blank spaces in their black books. I know that one of those spaces was awaiting my name.

You know, I can remember as far back as when I was age 10 when I became consciously aware that something different was taking place regarding my sexual nature. What I mean by this is that I began looking at guys in a different way, but I never made any advances toward any of them. I, however, had the experience of a guy making an advance toward me.

I was yet a pre-teen but my body didn't look like it. Physically I was looking somewhat older than my age because I was, as they say, "well endowed." I guess Andy thought that he could take the liberty of just coming up to me and proceed to fondle my breast. It happened so fast I didn't see him coming. As I was pushing him away he pushed me against the wall and started pressing against me. Sure, I got him off me. Then I ran away.

He had violated me! He had assumed that because my body looked mature that he had an automatic liberty to treat me as though I wanted to be with him sexually. Perhaps he thought that I was already sexually active.

Boy was he wrong! I was not active and did not want to be. I never intended to imply in any way that I was active. Still I felt something strange when he did what he did. My feelings scared me and increased my curiosity for what I had already seen, heard and read about. I knew from this point that I had better be careful about the way I carried myself, i.e. sit, walk, dress, etc. Guys seem to get the wrong ideas from innocence.

When I became a teenager I think I had an advantage. In my opinion I was not very attractive and I think I became a tomboy because I needed to hide my inferiority about my looks. I sought refuge through being a tomboy. The boys seemed to overlook me as a sexual interest and I was glad about that. During that time I became very obese due to overeating. As I think of it now, I think that overeating became my pacifier for the confusion I felt when I wanted answers as to why the boys were not interested in me. My inner emotions led me to grossly overeat. I guess being a virgin at that particular time in my life wasn't an issue, although it was yet a valuable virtue.

Around age fifteen I began experiencing a physical metamorphosis. I lost a considerable amount of weight, my skin became fairer, my hair grew, and my body formed into that of a woman. Suddenly out of nowhere there were phone calls, looks, stares, etc. from guys I hardly knew. You might say I was classified as an attractive, sexy young lady. Instinctively I could only hear guys say, I would love to be the first to have sex with you. Regardless to how many guys I met, I would hear the same thing. Boy did they ever miss it to think I would give up my virginity at fifteen. This is why I am praying that the world will embrace Chrissy and those like her who are willing to take a stand.

I had always thought that I would be a virgin until I got married. I am the firstborn of six children and was very conscientious about being the example. I was often referred to as "little miss perfect" and took it quite seriously. I went to an all-girls high school and did not have much experience with boys. I graduated from high school when I was almost sixteen and shortly thereafter found myself at an American university where most of my peers were 18+. By virtue of the fact that I came to America from another country, the cultural differences really scared me.

My time was divided between school and my personal life. Things started to look up when I met some natives from my country. I felt a freedom that was new to me. I enjoyed the fact that I had finally established friends who shared the same background as myself. There was finally someone with whom I could communicate.

Our group hung together for a long time. By the time I was 21 I was beginning to take interest in a young man in the group, Roger. He was fair-skinned, had curly hair, tall and just "awesome." He had a reputation for being a "ladies man." Despite his reputation I thought that if I could just go out with him that would be great. There was another guy in our group, David. David was my friend. When he realized that I was infatuated with Roger he tried to encourage me not to get involved. He told me the things I already knew and added the fact that Roger smoked ganja. I was too consumed with the fantasy that I had created about Roger to listen.

My infatuation was so strong that I began thinking of compromising my standard of waiting to have sex until I got married. As a matter of fact, Roger seemed to be a "Godsend." (I have repented of this error in perception.) I remember day-dreaming, thinking, wandering, being mesmerized by the idea of kissing Roger. I don't know if prior to this I had ever tried to kiss a boy in my entire life. If I had it must not have been anything because I cannot remember who, what, when, or where. If you want to put this situation in the form of a mathematical equation it would look like this:

Roger + me at age 21 and still a virgin + my desires + I was confused + I couldn't talk to my parents + there was no one else to share my private feelings with = me + do what I think in this matter.

I made one of the worst decisions of my life. Here's what happened:

One night Roger and I were at a birthday party. We had been spending a lot of time together. I can't remember how it happened but I agreed to go to his apartment afterwards to get something to eat. (He was going to cook for me.) We ate and later thought we would watch a movie in his bedroom. Shortly after the movie started the mood began to change. Roger began moving closer to me. Before I knew it he was asking me if this was my first time. I answered "yes." He said he would be gentle and walk me through it.

The problem with this type scenario is first, a young lady should never think that some sex-oriented, self-centered, egotistical guy with blank spaces in his black book could ever know or care about how important a woman's virginity is, especially to her future. While he was telling me that he would be gentle, I think that I needed to hear those words for an excuse to let down my guard. In the back of my mind I knew that regardless to how gentle he tried to be he could not be so gentle as to ease the pain of what I would have to face mentally, morally, emotionally, and psychologically. He was just saying what he had to say and what I wanted to hear. He was older than I was, slicker, and yes, a womanizer. Later I found out I was one out of a number of women who he had invited to his apartment, cooked a good meal and seduced to have sex.

I yielded my virginity to him and had what I thought was a special night. On the way home I was caught up in the moment reminiscing about the special time I had just had. As soon as I arrived home I began to have "reality thoughts." It was as though my fantasy bubble had burst. My mind started racing, "What have you done? You could be pregnant. How do you know that you aren't pregnant? I can't tell anyone. No one must find out!" I took a series of showers to try and make myself clean. I scrubbed frantically from head to toe. I was desperately seeking to cover my mistake.

The next day was Sunday and I went to church. I felt cheap, used, dirty, and stupid. I was struggling on the inside with how could I be a Christian professing salvation through Jesus and be in a situation such as this? I thought everyone could see through my façade and that they knew what I had done the night before. I made it through the day and headed for the university that evening.

Monday morning I was panic-stricken because I thought I was pregnant. I went to a clinic to try to get a morning after pill, the same pill they give to rape victims. I couldn't get one. On top of all that, I hadn't heard from Roger. I felt like I was one of the many girls that he had probably slept with just like David said. David tried to warn me.

Needless to say I did not get pregnant. Roger did call me but our friendship slowly became non-existent because sex was not going to be an active part of it. Even though I was 21when I lost my virginity, I felt like a 15 year-old because of my lack of experience with men. Ignorance about sex and men definitely proved to be a disadvantage for me.

Be careful about what you allow guys to say to you. It is not a "cool" thing to lose your virginity before marriage at any age. Contrary to what might be said today, having sex before marriage leaves a woman feeling like she has lost a part of herself that she will never be able to regain. Unfortunately, it is the exception rather than the rule that a man will respect you for giving in to the call of nature. Men have an innate need to feel a sense of kingship with each conquest. I see it today with so many men that I meet. It is in their attitude and their speech, but it is something that remains hidden and undiscovered unless you are looking for it.

Let me give you a bit of advice: Do not go into a sexual relationship blindly. Get the facts. Learn about sex and the emotional, physical and mental ramifications of such a relationship. Regardless of what others may say, the bottom line is abstinence before marriage is the best way to go. I hear people speak often of their sexual conquest as if it were a positive experience. This is not always true. When you ask others to be honest about their true feelings concerning these relationships you will find that the experience left them with insecurity and inferiority. There is generally something lacking within them that they have buried in the sexual experience.

Last but not least, there is the godly instruction regarding sex. Do not do it until you are married. The Bible gives specific instructions about sex and the do's and don'ts of it. If you follow the Word of God you will never go wrong. If you do happen to fall, there is instruction for that too. Given the same situation now with the knowledge I have obtained, the outcome would be different. Life would have taken a more positive turn for me. I would have been spared the lonely turmoil that I endured.

Again I want to encourage Chrissy and those like her that the standard that they have set is more precious than fine gold.

A PLEASANT DREAM TURNED NIGHTMARE

As a preteen, I made the decision to remain a virgin until I was married. I made this decision because I felt that it was pleasing to God. I remember this being taught in my Sunday school class.

Elementary school was not very hard for me regarding sex because I was actually a little tomboy and very active in sports. Being active in sports took up a great deal of my time.

Getting involved in constructive activities is a very good way to keep busy and not get caught up in the sex thing. Older people say that an idle mind is the devil's workshop.

High school, on the other hand, was very different for me. My classmates seemed to talk about sex more openly. (Or was it that I just had not been listening all of the other times?) I remember the conversations about sex making me uncomfortable. I would openly state my position about sex and make it known to whoever was in the conversation. My position was that I was a virgin and planned to stay that way until I married. Taking a stand about my desires and goals got many different responses. Some responses were encouraging, some were insulting and others were very challenging. The different responses brought a little discomfort because I knew what was right to do but that did not eliminate the pressure of joining the crowd.

Hold on to what you believe and don't let others change your mind, especially when the thing you are doing is pleasing to God.

Sometimes my peers would come to me and express their regrets about loosing their virginity and others would try to tell me how good it felt when they lost their virginity. My only question to the ones that expressed the joy of loosing their virginity was "Where was the joy?" They had times when they had to visit the doctor to take pregnancy tests and even had to be tested for sexually transmitted diseases (STDs).

Some of my friends complimented my actions and encouraged me to stay a virgin while others challenged my position as a virgin. Challenges came in many different forms. Girls would try and set me up with guys that were known for being sexually active. Guys would compliment me and ask me out on dates to see if they could be the first.

With girls and guys alike, make sure that you demand respect in your conversations. Don't allow people to talk to you about anything that makes you uncomfortable. If you know what your goal is stand on what you believe.

I made it through high school without having sex but I must admit that by the time I was a senior I had become increasingly interested in knowing what sex was like.

After finishing high school I had a lot of idle time. That was when I met Carlos. I liked him a lot and I allowed him to talk about sex with me. I allowed Carlos to say what I never allowed other guys to say to me about sex. Now that I think about it, I was more attracted to him than any other guy I had ever dated. He was cute and made me feel really gooey whenever I was near him. Because I felt that I was in love, I let my guard down and things began to happen in my life that I had never allowed before.

To make a long story short, I lost my virginity to Carlos during my first year of college. This was one act that changed my whole life. My goal to please God and not have sex until I was married was now a *pleasant dream turned nightmare.*

Galatians 6:9 plainly states, "And let us not be weary in well doing: for in due season we shall reap if we faint not."

This is one of my favorite scriptures however, it takes time for us to realize the power of the Word of God. Who would have ever believed the man that I was so attracted to, melted in his very presence, and most of all, lost my virginity to, would become physically abusive, egotistical, controlling, mean, hateful, uncaring, dirty, and a lowdown womanizer. If I sound angry and bitter I'm not but I will not cheat you out of the realities of this situation. I am now independent, strong and, thank God, away from the situation.

Sometimes I ask myself this question, "how could I have yielded my virginity to such a mean person? The answer is simply that I did not know that he was mean. All I saw was that he was cute and made me feel something very special. Add this to being young, and it equals making bad decisions that you will one day come to regret.

Watching Carlos develop stronger relationships with gay friends made me now wonder if the person that I was so in love with had not been infected with the AIDS virus. This has been the rumor. Although it has been many years since the termination of our relationship, I still sometimes fear having AIDS myself. I have been so afraid that I have been tested four times voluntarily. The results were negative! I don't have AIDS! Thank God!

This is the kind of stress that comes with making youthful and immature decisions like having sex. It's just not worth it to jeopardize your life for a moment of pleasure. In my case, it wasn't even that. I remember thinking, "What have I done? Why did I do it? Who am I now? How does he feel about me now?" If there was something to enjoy, my confusion killed it out. There were many times I felt used and abused and the one thing that I had as my trump card was now gone, my virginity! He had it. He used it, abused it and on top of that, he didn't marry me!!!! I cannot count the times he promised me that we would be married. All I ever dreamed of was marrying the man I gave my virginity to. Now I am awake to the reality that this dream never took place.

I am now a mother of two with no desire to marry Carlos. I love my children with all of my heart and would not trade them for the world. At the same time, I wish I had held on to my dream of not having sex until I was married.

Try everyday to please God with your life and remember that your goals are very important to you. You have not met your goals until all the requirements of your goals have been fulfilled.

I pray that my experience and hard-learned lesson will not be a hard-received message. To all readers, young and old, do not, under any circumstances, give to anyone your strength, dignity, chastity, morality, or your sexuality. I sit and think, while praising God, that God is the controller of my life's spirituality. I never thought that my experience would be a tool used to encourage and forewarn others.

I Corinthians 10:13 says, *There hath no temptation taken you but such as is common to man: but God is faithful, who will not suffer you to be tempted above that ye are able; but will with the temptation also make a way to escape that ye may be able to bear it.*

Romans 8:28 says, *All things work together for good to them that love the Lord....*

A VIRGIN MARRIAGE
(THE WIFE)

For me, being a virgin in a worldly society in the 80's was definitely challenging. This was true in high school and seemed to pose even more challenges as a college co-ed. The pressure from society to be sexually active was most prevalent and during that time casual sex seemed to be at an all time high, in spite of the growing knowledge of AIDS, Chlamydia, Herpes and other STDs. It seemed that every time you turned on the TV you were faced with the media's emphasis on the notion that "everybody's doing it." (I have to stop and encourage all young people to know, everybody is not doing it!)

I was constantly forced to counsel myself to stick to my convictions in spite of the fact that many guys' interest often dwindled when they found out that I was waiting until after marriage to begin that facet of life. I wanted more than anything to complete my life's goals and as near as I could tell, having a baby before marriage would definitely ruin my plans. I also felt that I owed my parents more than that type of repayment after all they had done for me. I knew that they had raised me right. I am not judgmental of anyone who made that mistake, but I felt it was one that I could not afford to make.

When I turned 21, I found a deeper commitment to Christ and I knew I would then have the help of the Word of God and the Holy Ghost to keep me. More important than my personal goals and pleasing my parents was pleasing God.

Temptations do not change because of a declared commitment to Christ. However, with everything in you, you have to flee fornication and youthful lusts. If you do not flee, you may get caught. Staying in the scriptures, fasting and praying is a must. Even when you are at your greatest spiritual height, temptations come. Even when you are dating another believer with the same convictions, as I was, (and if you are a believer, that should be the case) the temptations are there. However, if you are in agreement, you can walk together and help each other. That is why it is necessary not to get caught in compromising positions. I'm only saying this so that you are not deceived. Getting caught in dark, close places is too close for spiritual comfort. Do not lose your conviction by ignoring the Lord's voice. My pastor teaches that any bit of intimacy, no matter how small it may seem, opens the flesh up to a desire for yet a deeper level of intimacy. I have found this to be true. When you are involved with someone sexually, you become one with that person, and if God has not put you together, you open yourself up to spiritual and emotional problems you will not be able to handle.

Having waited, I feel that my marital relationship has a level of trust that may not have otherwise been there. You see I was 25 years old when I married. My husband and I were both virgins. From day one of our marriage I knew that what we had was very special.

I would advise anyone to make up your mind and take a stand for Christ in spite of the Prince Charmings you meet. In the end you will be glad. Remember, <u>until he says, "I do" let him know that you don't.</u> If God sent him, he will wait.

A VIRGIN MARRIAGE
(THE HUSBAND)

In all of my thoughts and opinions on premarital sex, I never imagined that the reward for saving myself until marriage would culminate in my finding the perfect mate. I also never thought that I would have the opportunity to write an excerpt in a potential bestseller. When I look back over my life I can truly say that the Lord kept me in a commitment that I made to remain a virgin until I was married. I say it was the Lord because honestly, I don't know what exactly prompted me to want to wait. I grew up in the same type of environment, with the enticements and vices that others encountered. Just in case you want to know, there was tremendous pressure on me to give in. For some reason, I wanted my first time to be special and not just any woman would do. It had to be that special lady that I wanted to have more than a physical relationship with. I must admit that the road wasn't easy and there were times when I didn't think I would make it, but by the grace of God I believe I was chosen as an example.

I remember the times that I wanted to give in and if the moment would have presented itself I probably would have. I am very thankful that in the times when I was weak the temptation wasn't there. I'm also thankful that when the moments along with the temptation came, either conviction or my being chicken overrode my desires and I was saved for the moment. I mentioned pressure earlier and what I meant was that the ways of the world were changing.

There was a time when pre-marital sex was unacceptable; I didn't say it wasn't happening. Growing up in the era that I came up in, the late 70's and 80's, things began changing and pre-marital sex was becoming more accepted among the young as well as the old.

Many of the pressures I faced came from within as well as from the outside. My inward pressures were the results of growing into the adolescent years when sexuality begins to take its place in your life and of course being intrigued with the growth and development of the female body. Outside pressures came from older teenagers as well as my peers who made it seem as if you didn't have it going on if you were a virgin. I tell you it was tough because at the time, I didn't have Christ. I was feeling things inwardly that I had never felt before and the worldly pressures made me feel as if I were wrong for wanting to wait.

Well, I made it through Junior-High and High school but I wasn't always honest about my virginity. It seemed the older I got the more ashamed I became. When I graduated from High School, I went into the military. I joined to get away from home and to possibly partake in some of the wild happenings I had heard stories about. The wild happenings never took place because at the ripe old age of 18 I made a serious commitment to make Jesus the Lord of my life. What a relief I felt. It was as though I had been rescued. Not necessarily from my natural desires, but I was now in a different world and my position as a virgin was very much accepted. It was then that I realized that sexuality was a beautiful thing that served many purposes and that it shouldn't be looked at or indulged in, in a casual or irresponsible way. I also realized that I didn't have to be ashamed because I was a virgin. It should be those who opt to not be virgins that should be ashamed. To tell you the truth one day when I was reading the bible I came to a scripture that said the world's system would make you think that living a righteous life is wrong. Wow! That blew me away because I recognized then that the world would call wrong right and right wrong. That scripture fortified my stand and it strengthened me to fight on.

There were several things that helped me make it through my military years. First there was Christ. My environment changed and the word of God was my strength. I had saved friends and we constantly encouraged one another. Secondly, there was fear and lastly there was the fact that I didn't have a girlfriend. There was one other thing that was pressure filled to me, finding someone who was a virgin. Don't get me wrong; I was willing not to be choosy because I know its not easy finding virgins these days. I am not so naïve as to think that every person willingly gave up their virginity; Some others were forced due to various circumstances or violations that may have taken place in their lives. Still, deep on the inside I wanted someone just like me. I wanted a virgin because I didn't want to have to think about how many partners she may have had. Also with my being inexperienced, I would not have to worry about having to compete sexually with a past lover when we were having a moment of intimacy.

In 1987 I met and began dating a very beautiful and virtuous young lady. Just in our conversation I knew that she was the one for me. When she told me that she was a virgin, I was very excited and I wasn't ashamed to tell her that I was also. We were married in 1991 and at the age 27, I lost my virginity. I couldn't think of a better way to lose it. There was no guilt, only a feeling of peace and relief. I thank God for a mate with whom I am sexually compatible and I tell you every time we share in a moment of intimacy it is just as special as the first time. I remember a year or so ago I saw a billboard that read, "Parents, teach your kids that *virgin* is not a dirty word." I would like to leave a word of encouragement to the readers. Young ladies don't worry, there are still some good young men and young men there are still some virtuous young ladies as well. Remember, you don't have to be ashamed, because you are special.

A MALE EXAMPLE

My name is Johnny, bka (better known as), Puppy Dog. I am now 31 years old. I have been happily married for more than 10 years. I have never experienced having sex with but one woman, my wife. I feel very proud that this is my testimony. I learned how to cope with the image and false accusation of being a *sissy* or a *slow goer* just because I was sexually inactive. I guess I could have been sexually active. I was handsome, smart, like most other guys. However, I had an experience that kicked me into gear and opened my eyes to what this sex thing could do.

During my teenage years there was a very special person in my life whom I was very close to and really admired. I thought he was pretty cool until I found out that he had gotten three women pregnant and all three pregnancies ended with abortions. This was devastating and very painful for me to hear. That's when I decided as a teen that if sex meant abortion then I was not going to participate. Although I was just a teenager I personally could not bear the pain of thinking how easily someone could destroy life just because they wanted to satisfy their sexual nature. There was not a reason good enough to be loose and take having an abortion so lightly. I wonder about those aborted babies. Who were they? What would they have become had they been given a chance to live?

I admit that it was hard for me to be celibate (sexually inactive). I was a normal child with natural desires as well. However if I am ever known for anything in life, I wish to be known for this proverb, "What I wanted was more powerful than what I felt I was missing through sex."

We are in the 21st century and even now when I tell my friends that I was a virgin until marriage, male friends look at me as if I had missed something. You know the "Oh you don't know what you are missing" look or the "Oh really you've got to be kidding." There is also that "How did you make it with so many pretty aggressive girls around?'

What's wrong with our society? How did we get so reversed, with such double standards? Why do we treat doing right and being moral as if it is wrong? Why do we act as though only women can be virgins and if there is a man that is a virgin he should be ashamed of himself? This is not what God wants from us. Men, do not feel neglected because you have not experienced sex. Also, I have not experienced the guilt of encouraging a girl to have an abortion because of my irresponsibility, AIDS, STDs and most of all a loss of my standard and values.

My mother raised me with morals and values and I believe that they are yet important. I am not embarrassed at meeting a status quo that many men do not desire. I feel special and powerful in that I could contain and control my sexual desires.

I do believe that if I had fornicated before marriage it would have been easy for me to commit adultery during marriage. To not fornicate is to be committed to morals and values, therefore making a commitment to an individual much easier. The fact that I didn't fornicate makes me proud to say that I have a clean slate, a happy marriage and a wonderful wife. I think that she is one of God's special creatures. She thinks I am a little crazy. (Smile honey.)

Do men ever stop to think what women feel when they are forced to have an abortion? Probably not. Why should they care? All they want is sex. Many men do not want marriage or to be fathers, and they definitely do not want the responsibility of raising a child.

Do not let anyone tell you that you must be gay if you are a man and a virgin. That is not the case. It wasn't for me and it will not be for you. I am happy to be so special to have only been with one woman. This is an honor to me. I want young men to follow my example. Some will laugh at my story when they read it. They may read my story and laugh at me and mock me with their friends. I only hope that those who do mock will not be given the selfish pleasure of messing up some young girl's life. There are just too many irresponsible men in the world today.

Why do we get mad enough at people to want to murder them, but we don't; desire to drive at unsafe high speeds, but we don't (I must admit that it is my desire to become a race car driver); want to tell our parents off, but we don't; want to hit the policeman that stops us for no reason, frisks us and takes us down, but we don't? It is because we know the consequences. When it comes to sex we have heard and read the consequences but we do not regard them. Going to the doctor and getting penicillin should not be the easy answer to our lack of responsibility. Some reading my story have already contracted HIV. Is that you? Is your answer no because you don't really know? Allow me to use this example:

You have the AIDS virus but you are unaware of it because there are no outward signs. You do not have any concern above sexual satisfaction so your activity is growing every week. Your partners have absolutely no idea that you have the AIDS virus so how can they protect themselves? The answer is they can't. This is not far out nor far fetched, it happens nearly every day. Selfish people without morals and a standard jeopardize other people's lives. Men especially, are known for this (forgive me if I sound bias).

I want young men to be responsible. Run from the suggestion that "if you are a man and a virgin you are gay." This is not true, more so it is very honorable and pleasing to God.

I want to thank Chrissy for the opportunity to write a part in this very powerful and much needed book. Keep up the good work young lady. I'll just chill now and allow you to respond.

Wow, what a testimony, thank you Puppy Dog for your story. It has helped me to realize that not all men are selfish and self-centered. It is rewarding to know how you feel about abortions and that there may be other young men who feel the same. As a society we are led to believe differently. I am very impressed with this storyline. There must have been a lot of pressure but not so much that you gave up your standard. You are so cool, Puppy Dog! Thank you for your example. We need more men just like you. To me you are an example of true manhood because you are responsible and smart. Your wife must be honored to have you. I'm sure that she is a very special lady. Your mother receives a reward for instilling within you those kinds of principles. You seem to be proud to say that you have only been with one woman, which is contrary to this world's way of thinking. I find it honorable that you are not too embarrassed to admit to it.

To those who are virgins and you are reading this story remember that you are special to this world. I wonder what men who are not chaste and have no morals, those who trained themselves to think that sex was so important and are now in jail with a room full of the same sex, do now? I mean there are no women around to abuse. Do they just turn off their sexuality or trade partners? If the answer is, I do not trade partners nor can I turn it off, then this book is to encourage others to remember someone else is following you. Try to help them so that they will not make your same mistake.

God forgives all our sins. You can start over. Decide to be celibate from this point on since God does not charge our past to us. You can become a new creature ("Therefore if any man be in Christ, he is a new creature: old things are passed away; behold, all things are become new." II Corinthians 5:17) You can actually teach others where not to go and what not to do, explaining to them the pain that goes with supporting abortion, the disease factors, and most of all the lies that are told at the price of self-satisfaction. As I'm sure Puppy Dog would put it, get a job, be responsible for your personal life and then you are prepared to get married and have sex.

SAFE SEX   OR   NO SEX?

This is not good. Statistically speaking, 6 in 10 pregnancies occur among teenagers who are 18-19 years old. In 1997, over 10,000 girls in Georgia, ages 10 to 17, became pregnant; nearly 800 of these were under 15 years old (DHR Division of Public Health). The AIDS epidemic is spreading faster among people under age 24 than in any other age group. HIV is spreading quickly in many rural areas, especially in the south, and the increase in female adolescents is among the highest (Youth Law News, May-June 1995).

These statistics are so unfortunate considering the money that our society has poured into campaigning for the use of contraceptives and the emphasis placed on "safe sex."   Do you think that this may be the problem? The emphasis is placed on encouraging teens to go ahead and have sex but just make sure that they take measures to prevent conception and the spread of disease by *keeping it safe.* Why are we talking contraceptives and *safe sex*? Why are we not talking abstinence? With the resources that we have available through the media, government funding, private organizations, empowerment programs, etc., it seems that as a nation we could do a much better job promoting sexual abstinence among our young people. Although reports show that there has been a decline in the teen pregnancy rate over the last decade, still there are too many babies having babies.

The fact is, as a nation we have accomplished the great feat of sending men to the moon. We can now communicate across the world almost at the speed of thought via the internet, but we are crippled when it comes to developing programs that will assist in the prevention of teen pregnancy and help young people to become more productive citizens and less reproductive in the early years of their lives.

Fourteen years of my working career was with the local Department of Family and Children Services (DFCS). Working for DFCS was more than an interesting experience for me; it was a dose of reality. It was sad watching pregnant, unwed teens waddle into my office to apply for government checks. It became an everyday occurrence. Girls would see their visit to the "Welfare Office" as no more than an opportunity to "receive their own check." Many would often ask at the close of our interview, "Does this mean that I can now get my own check?" The reason for this question was that they did not wish to be included in their mother's family group; they wanted to be a separate family. Checks were distributed to individual families; this was how it was in order to get your "own" check. For the teen mother, she would have her own check. This meant that the individual would have her own money.

For many teens *getting your own check* meant that they would have money that they could spend in the way that they chose. With this in mind it was not long before they realized that the more children they had the more money they could receive. The increase in the check amount was sometimes the deciding factor between having another baby and being content with the existing check amount.

When I was first hired with DFCS I thought that I would be helping people that perhaps were a little less fortunate than myself. It wasn't until about five years of being employed there that I realized that I was promoting teen pregnancy in an odd sort of way. You see, every time I approved an application for assistance, especially to a teenager, it seemed as though I was rewarding her for having a baby. Not only that, I was aiding her in becoming codependent upon a system that I felt would eventually fail. And it did.

For many years after realizing that I was working in a professional capacity that was doing our children more harm than good, I encouraged teens to strive to do more with their lives than settle for birthing babies by boys who were yet babies themselves. The *Welfare System* as we had come to know it began changing rapidly. The United States Congress enacted laws that required welfare recipients to go to work. Limitations were placed on the amount that an individual could receive and a cap was placed on the number of years that a person could get assistance.

While this was a pretty difficult adjustment to make for many of my clients nevertheless it was the way things were. I must say that I was glad to see these changes becoming effective. The main reason that I say this is because despite the sad stories of teenage pregnancy many teens were not getting the right message. Allow me to share a few stories with you:

Once I took an application on a 17-year old girl who was pregnant. Her baby was due any day. When she first walked into my office I was sorry to see that her application indicated that she had dropped out of high school. Not only was she a dropout but she also had two other children. Here she was pregnant with her third child and she was still a child! She had her first child when she was 13-years old and her second child at the age of 15. There she was, 17 and pregnant with her third child. At the rate that she was going she was destined to have another child at the age of 19 if things did not change. It really grieved me to know that in working with DFCS I was in essence encouraging her to have more babies. I mean, I may not have okayed it in my conversation, but in a few short days she was going to be rewarded for having another baby, and I could not do anything about it. Young person, when you have your first child it is easier to have a second one within a couple years. According to statistics ¼ of teenage mothers have a second child within 2 years of their first.

This was not an isolated story. Many times while working with DFCS I found myself consoling parents of teenagers who were pregnant and confused. I once had a mother (whom I will call Ms. Jones for the sake of this story) to come in with her 13-year-old daughter (let's just call her Kelly) to apply for assistance. Kelly had never told her mother that she was pregnant. Due to the fact that Kelly was over-weight her mother had no suspicion that her daughter was pregnant. One day Ms. Jones came home from work to find Kelly doubled over in pain. When asked what was wrong, Kelly replied that she thought that she had eaten something that did not agree with her. Seeing the look on her child's face Ms. Jones decided to take no chances. Could her child have appendicitis or some terrible stomach virus? Hurriedly she raced Kelly to the hospital. After a very long wait in the hospital's emergency room, the doctor finally came out to address Ms. Jones.

The first thing that he said was that it was good that she had gotten Kelly to the hospital when she did because she nearly went into shock. The next thing that he said was, "the mother and child are just fine." Mother and child? Yes, in her episode of anguish, Kelly was in labor with Ms. Jones' first grandchild. Ms. Jones had no idea that Kelly had a case of *pregnancy*.

Why is this story not raising your eyebrow? This scenario has become too familiar to our society and no longer surprising. I'm sorry to see that society has become numb to these type situations. Something has to be done.

The last story I would like to share is the other side of being young, unwed and pregnant. Most of the teens that I interviewed had very little knowledge of the child's father. Often the only name they knew was a nickname. Even if they did know the father of their child, the relationship between the two of them had gone sour the moment he was told that she was pregnant. Many young men did not want to be parents they just intended to have a little fun. When challenged with the question of whether the child could be his child, the average young man would deny that he even knew the child's mother. He would insist that the young girl was lying on him. Due to the gross immaturity of the people involved there was also a great lack of responsibility toward parenting the child. I witnessed so many young girls feeling hurt because they were lied to and told, "I love you" by some boy who did not know what love was.

Many teenage girls are not aware that they are a part of a game that boys play to see how many girls they can get to have sex with them so that they can brag to their friends. For the average sexually active young man, it is about statistics; how many girls can they actually say they have "been with?"

The reason that this saddens me is because I feel that every young person should be given a chance to make the best of life. Having children at an early age, for many teens, inhibits any future ambition of completing school, going to college, traveling and exploring the great things that life has to offer. It's not that life ends when you have children at an early age but the statistics don't lie. When teens have children many times they increase the illiteracy rate, the dropout rate, the numbers of those living at poverty level, etc.

Having sex is an adult thing that should occur between two individuals who are married to one another. The fact that television programs and movies applaud sex outside of marriage makes the battle of communicating this truth very difficult. We are in a war trying to bring children back to a responsibly moral lifestyle.

You know, it was only about thirty years ago that women and men took great care to not scar their relationship by becoming sexually active before marriage. A woman who cared about her name would not spend time with a man without being in a controlled environment, i.e. dating as a group, courting at her home with a specific time that the young man had to leave, etc. Even when it came time to marry, the young man would ask the young lady if she would marry him and he would courteously write her parents for permission to have their daughter's hand in marriage. Most of the time the letter would be written to her father if he were still living. Now there is so much emphasis placed on getting sexually involved without being married. This occurs before the individuals even get a chance to know one another.

Never do you hear the characters in the leading soap operas state what a disappointment the sexual experience was in the last scene. That's because this thing called *sex* is so overrated that it is actually glorified through many media sources. *Sex* can be a major disappointment if the people involved are not prepared for the real deal. It should be the moral responsibility of every adult to give children a chance to mature and develop emotionally, mentally, spiritually and sexually. This should be done without interruption or interference. The mere suggestion that two people should become intimately involved without even considering consequences is ludicrous. This type of behavior must stop.

The next time that you are faced with the decision to become sexually indulgent first stop and think. Ask yourself, "Is this what I want to do? Am I ready to risk having to cope with STDs, pregnancy, loneliness from being a statistic in someone's little black book, raising a child without a father, etc.? How will this one time involvement affect the rest of my life?" Be real with yourself and remind yourself that *virgin is not a dirty word.*

Thanks Chrissy, for allowing me to have a part in this wonderful book. I hope that your mission to get other young people to do as you are doing will be the greatest success. God bless.

HEALING SECTION

In this section of the book I am going to need help. Because I realize just how serious this section is, I have asked the help of my father and my big sister and mentor, Precious. I am proud of the fact that the three of us had input in this section. Due to the fact that I would not know what to say to help you in your healing I needed the help of those who do know what to say. Besides, I do not have my degree in psychology yet. (You didn't know?)

My father is an experienced counselor and powerfully anointed church leader. He has written the following information with the hope of providing healing for those who are yet experiencing the guilt of their past sexual encounter(s). Thank you, Dad. That's just like you, always wanting to help others. I want to be just like you. He is going to write for the three of us so let me yield my pen to him. Take it away Dad.

Thank you Chrissy. Baby, Daddy does realize that you have homework, chores, church activities, driving lessons, shopping, career, and many "parrot/ smoke-type" situations (you know what I mean☺), going on in your life, not to mention the difficult task of writing this book. I'll do my best to represent you. Let's get started.

This section of the book is written strictly for the purpose of healing. I believe that it would be blatant negligence on my behalf as a pastor to not take advantage of this opportunity to minister healing to those to whom this scenario may apply. I realize that there are many reading this book that will ask the question, "What do I do with the fact that I was raped, molested or violated and, in my opinion, am no longer a virgin?" Perhaps you were molested, raped or taken advantage of at a young age, whatever the situation, even if consensual, you can find healing for your inner self.

First, let me say that I'm sorry if this unfortunate fate has befallen you. "Life may not be clear but it is fair" (James S.

Prothro, *Man, God's Robot*). Later in this section I am going to introduce a concept called *secondary virginity* which I feel will be quite beneficial to those who are bearing the burden of guilt. It is my desire to encourage you to wipe your tears. You have not lost your virginity if you have not <u>willfully</u> and with <u>voluntary consent</u> given it away. <u>Pure virginity is based on virtue.</u>

Many virtuous people may not be virgins by definition because they were taken advantage of. However, the person(s) who violated their virginity can never violate their virtue, thank God. Although you may have been the individual who was violated and maybe your perpetrator physically and/or mentally overpowered you via some forceful means or through some conning means, he could not take your virtue from you. Based on the scriptures it is safe to assume that in God's eyes you have remained a virgin.

If a person cut your finger off would you still be human? Of course you would and if you have been raped and intercourse took place, you still have not willfully given your virginity away. Therefore you should do your best to try and live without the guilt of feeling as if you have sinned when in actuality, sin was committed against you.

When an individual is forced to engage in a sexual experience without agreeing to do so, the guilt upon the victim of that experience should be equal to that of visiting the doctor. Never should we feel guilty that our physician has examined our "private parts" to ensure that we are healthy. Though the examination may require some form of manipulation of the genitalia there is no sexual stimulation because that is not the purpose for being there. In this case manipulation of your private parts does not constitute a loss of your virtue and virginity. Although there are times when many will leave the doctor's office feeling embarrassed, still few will feel that they are no longer a virgin because of an exam. An individual must have the intent to willfully engage in a sexual act, both mind and body, for that act to be consensual. Anything else is violation and should not be considered loss of virginity.

In the Webster's Third New International Dictionary, the word *virgin* is defined as free of impurity. When someone violates you it doesn't make you impure, only you can do that. Do not let the fact that, you were unable to prevent being violated cause you to take upon yourself the freedom of sexual promiscuity. Keep your virtue, chastity and your self-respect. Maintain your chastity and you will protect your virginity. The picture of what happened to you may be ever so clear in your mind but if you are free from granting permission for the act to occur then you should not take the blame. In other words imagine if you were addressing your perpetrator and you asked him this question, "If you had not violated me would I have invited you?" If the answer is, "no" then I'm very proud to be writing this on your behalf.

When we use the word *impure,* we mean, to be unchaste. Do you think that you are no longer a chaste, virtuous and moral person because you were violated? As a matter of fact, neither do I. God has designed our lives so that only what we allow are we accountable for. (Praise God!)

Please, learn to forgive your violator. I highly recommend my book, *Water For Dry Seasons*, to aid you in your efforts to forgive. Talk to a competent authorized counselor who can help you stand up and be counted as a virgin. Tell the devil, "Your violations do not cancel my virginity because it did not touch my virtue." Virtue comes from God and what God gives no one else can take. Be healed and enjoy your virginity.

Apostle James S. Prothro

SECONDARY VIRGINITY

So you made a mistake, did you? It happened so quickly that you had done it without realizing the consequences. Yes, it is true that we reap what we sow; however, nothing can chastise or whip the individual who loses their virginity, like the inner self-conscience.

We all make mistakes. It's not so bad that we make mistakes, what's bad is what we plan to do about our mistakes. Remember that old cliché "Ain't no use cryin' over spilled milk." If you waste the milk and stand there crying and pouting about it, it is not going to do anything but sour and ruin the carpet. If you have made a mistake by losing your virginity, there's no use in pouting and talking about it, or condemning yourself for being a terrible person while worrying that your family and friends may feel the same. You just need to clean up what has been messed up, and I don't mean with paper towels, as some people might do when they spill milk. You clean up by repenting and freeing yourself from guilt.

Let me give you two important scriptures that I feel may help you to understand what I am saying: Romans 8:1 *There is therefore now no condemnation to them which are in Christ Jesus, who walk not after the flesh, but after the Spirit.* II Corinthians 5:17 *Therefore if any man be in Christ, he is a new creature: old things are passed away; behold, all things are become new.*

How much of what you have done do you think God holds you responsible for? You should not be foolish neither hypocritical in your answer. From the point of repenting and freeing yourself of guilt you must commit to changing and doing better. With that said, allow me to introduce the concept of *secondary virginity*. *Secondary virginity* is the act of becoming a virgin again. It is established when an individual commits to the practice of abstinence while assuring themselves that they will not repeat the same action.

Don't just think that saying you're going to be a *secondary virgin* is good enough. Do not try convincing yourself that you have changed by adjusting your dress code, i.e. wearing longer dresses. You must truly believe that you can become a *secondary virgin*. If you do this then you can regain your virginity and dignity. Remember you will have to commit to abstinence and mean it in your heart. Your commitment is not established via what you say with your lips but what you determine in your heart.

In the Word of God we read that, when we are in Christ Jesus "old things are passed away and behold all things are become new." What a wonderfully powerful verse of scripture. It is so comforting to know that God does not hold our mistakes against us, and neither should we. He forgives those who lose their virginity regardless of age or reason. To Him, the reason for why we lost our virginity is not important, rather, what we do about it.

Secondary virginity requires your commitment to celibacy and abstinence. Thank God that you can! From your past experience you are more knowledgeable of the consequences, this leaves you in control. Your renewed commitment can make you feel as if you are being hypocritical. I don't think so. I think that as long as you are honest with yourself and admit to having made a mistake then you are accepting responsibility for your mistakes. You must pick up the pieces of your life and go on.

Being a virgin has more to do with chastity, virtue and morality than sexuality. By the phrase *secondary virgin*, I'm basically trying to tell you that you can start again. I know, technically, you can't physically become a virgin again. Although this is true, I also know that mentally, spiritually, morally and with chastity, you can. When you first come to realize that God forgives, you will then be able to realize that what everyone else thinks really doesn't matter.

There are many people who have been molested, raped, etc. Do you think that their fate has erased their opportunity to remain a virgin? Well, it doesn't. It does mean that they must address the issue that physically something occurred. What about the rest of themselves, i.e. mind, spirit, etc.? Again they must resolve to do something. Why not resolve to get started again? Yes, again. If they would say within themselves, "I did nothing to be ashamed of. God has forgiven others and He has forgiven me." Even though forgiveness may not be necessary, exoneration of guilt may be necessary for the individual.

I would like to propose this question to those who were not raped or violated, but were perhaps willing participants. If a man is a drunkard, a gambler or a murderer and the Lord saves him, is he known by what he was? No! He may testify of what he used to do yet he is still not known by what he used to do. What makes him different is the words expressed in II Corinthians 5:17, *Therefore if any man be in Christ, he is a new creature: old things are passed away; behold, all things are become new.*

I do not believe that God is going to see that person as an ex-drunkard or ex-murderer, but rather a newborn creature. The same is true with the loss of one's virginity. In the eyes of God it was an act of fornication or adultery make no doubt about it. Still when he forgives, He relieves the one forgiven of the guilt within the sin. In other words, regardless to what's going on, we are forgivable and God is forgiving. (Now ain't that good news?) You can take your past mistakes and learn from them. Do not let your past errors condemn you. You can still be a virgin.

Let me ask you some challenging questions that will demand your truthfulness and honesty. What are your present actions? Are you practicing abstinence? Are you a morally chaste and virtuous person? If a person is a virgin it should mean that they are not sexually active. It can also mean that they are non-active because they choose rather to be chaste, moral and virtuous.

Many assume that once your virginity is lost it is gone forever. However, as I have made it clear already, I choose to think just a little differently. There are different reasons why people lose their virginity and some of those reasons have been introduced to you in this book. There are those who were violated by means of rape or molestation. Also those who lost their virginity because they thought they were in love. However, no matter how you lost your virginity, there is a way to regain that title of VIRGIN.

I would like to briefly share a scenario of a girl who was violated at the age of eleven. We can all agree that there was no way that she was old enough to know what was going on. Although she blamed herself, it was not her fault. Due to the innocence of her role in the situation, in that it was not her will for the act to take place, in actuality it was more of a violation than loss of virginity. Being a virgin means more than just being inexperienced sexually. It is also defined as an unmarried woman who has religious vows of chastity. It further means, being in a pure or natural state. Thus you see why I say that you can be a virgin again. That child could not decide for herself to be a nonvirgin. Her youthfulness and the purity of her innocence will prevail over her physical loss of virginity. As she gets older she will learn from that experience how to be chaste and pure in what she does.

Here's another scenario. Let's look at the young woman who was a virgin until age 21. When she lost her virginity she really was considered grown, thus responsible enough to make her own decisions. (Please know that I am not at all saying that premarital sex at any age is okay, but she was an adult and able to handle her mistakes better than those who are much younger.) She thought that she loved the guy with whom she had become intimate and she thought that he loved her. Although in her mind she questioned what she was doing, what she was feeling in her body overrode what she thought in her mind. Now that she is much older, she looks in retrospect at what she did and has made a personal pledge to save herself until marriage. This is another example of why I believe there is such a thing as a *secondary virgin*.

As young people, you should learn to always do what you think is right, and if it turns out that you have made a mistake, learn from it. Try not to ever regret anything that has happened in your life because, life affords us an array of experiences (James S. Prothro). This means you will experience many things, some good and some bad but all of it can be handled. Of course, there are those experiences that you wish had not happened, however, through all of your experiences, you should grow and become a better person. The things that you have learned should all be sifted and applied to your life as needed. Here is what I mean:

A person who is miserable and mad because they have lost their virginity will create a beautiful picture about their sexual experience in order to make you feel as though you are missing out. They may tell you that sex is something that it's not. They will try to make you think that you will regret your decision to remain a virgin. Things like this should be ignored. Please, young people, don't allow what others say about their experience to persuade you. Again, I say, I wholeheartedly believe that there are *secondary virgins*, however, I believe that it is best to stay a virgin from the *jump street* (the beginning).

To those who are still virgins, continue to maintain your purity. Wait on marriage. To those who have perhaps made some mistakes, remember that God has forgiven you and now I want you to forgive yourself and come on back to the *Virgin's Island*. To lose your virginity because of your own curiosity and at your own will is still no reason to think that you cannot restore yourself. You must decide that you want to become a virgin again. I'm sure that many feel that this is an absurd concept, but remember, it's all about what you want to do. Make up your mind to become pure again, make a vow to yourself and know that you can restore yourself and be whoever you want to be. You can become a *secondary virgin*.

VICES VERSUS VIRGINITY
IT'S YOUR CHOICE

Sexually Transmitted Diseases (STDs) are infections that are transferred by sexual intercourse; *virgins do not have this to worry about.*

Sexually Transmitted Diseases Statistics

- In the United States, more than 12 million new cases of sexually transmitted diseases (STDs) occur each year, at least 3 million of them among teenagers.[1]

- Of the top 10 reportable diseases in the United States in 1995, four are STDs (chlamydial infection, gonorrhea, AIDS, and syphilis).[2]

- **Approximately two-thirds of people who acquire STDs in the United States are younger than 25.**[1]

- Worldwide, an estimated 333 million new cases of four curable STDs (gonorrhea, chlamydial infection, syphilis and trichomoniasis) occurred among adults 15 to 49 years of age in 1995.[3]

- The World Bank has estimated that STDs, excluding AIDS, are the second leading cause of healthy life lost among women between ages 15 to 44 in the developing world.[4]

Various Types of Diseases

1) **HIV/AIDS**----The cumulative number of AIDS cases reported to CDC is 733,374. Adults and adolescent AIDS cases total 724,656 with 604,843 cases in males and 119,810 cases in females. Through the same time period, 8,718 AIDS cases were reported in children under age 13. Total deaths of persons reported with AIDS are 430,441, including 425,357 adults and adolescents, and 5,084 children under age 13.

- As of December 1997, an estimated 30.6 million people worldwide were living with HIV/AIDS. Cumulative AIDS-related deaths worldwide as of December 1997 numbered approximately 11.7 million.[5]

- In 1997 alone, HIV/AIDS-associated illnesses caused the deaths of approximately 2.3 million people worldwide.[5]

- In the United States, 612,078 cases of AIDS had been reported to the Centers for Disease Control and Prevention (CDC) as of June 30, 1997. Of these people, 379,258 had died by the end of June 1997.[6]

- In 1994, the total cost of sexually transmitted HIV infection in the United States was approximately $6.7 billion.[1]

2) Chlamydial Infection

- Infection with *Chlamydia trachomatis* is the most common bacterial STD in the United States. More than 4 million new cases are estimated to occur annually, including 2.6 million cases among women.[1]

- From 1987 to 1996, the annual reported rate of chlamydial infections in the United States increased 406 percent (from 48 to 195 cases per 100,000).[7]

- Worldwide, an estimated 89 million new chlamydial infections occurred in 1996.

- If not adequately treated, 20 to 40 percent of women with genital chlamydial infections develop pelvic inflammatory disease (PID), which in turn causes problems such as infertility, ectopic pregnancy and chronic pelvic pain.[1]

3) Gonorrhea

- An estimated 800,000 cases of gonorrhea, caused by *Neisseria gonorrhoeae*, occur annually in the United States.[1]

- In 1996, 325,883 cases of gonorrhea in the United States were reported to the CDC, a case rate of 124/100,000.[7]

- Approximately 50 percent of *N. gonorrhoea* infections in women are asymptomatic.

- Worldwide, an estimated 62 million new cases of gonorrhea occurred in 1996.[9]

- If not adequately treated, 10 to 40 percent of women infected with gonorrhea develop PID.[1]

4) Pelvic Inflammatory Disease (PID)

- At least 1 million cases of PID, an important complication of both gonorrhea and chlamydial infection, occur annually in the United States.[1]

- Of all infertile women, at least 15 percent are infertile because of tubal damage caused by PID.[1]

- Following PID, scarring will cause approximately 20 percent of women to become infertile, 18 percent to develop chronic pelvic pain, and 9 percent to have ectopic pregnancies.[8]

5) Genital Herpes

- About one in five people in the United States over age 12 - approximately 45 million individuals - are infected with the virus that causes genital herpes.[9]

6) Hepatitis B

- An estimated 53,000 cases of sexually transmitted hepatitis B infection occurred in the United States in 1994.[1]

7) Syphilis

- An estimated 101,000 sexually transmitted infections with *Treponema pallidum*, the cause of syphilis, occur each year in the United States; in addition, approximately 3,400 newborns acquire the infection from their mothers before or during birth.[1]

- Globally, an estimated 12 million new cases of sexually acquired syphilis occurred in 1996.[9]

- In 1996, 11,387 cases of primary and secondary syphilis in the United States were reported to the CDC, a case rate of 4.3/100,000. The rate of reported syphilis cases among African Americans was nearly 50 times greater than that among whites.[7]

8) Trichomoniasis

- Globally, an estimated 170 million people acquired *Trichomonas vaginalis*, a sexually transmitted parasite, in 1996 (WHO).[9]

- Approximately 3 million cases of trichomoniasis occurred in the United States in 1994.[1]

STDs Defined

Although some of these diseases are less well-known in the United States than others they are still important. Some are especially significant for pregnant women. Many of these infections are of serious concern for people in other parts of the world, particularly in developing countries.

Pubic Lice

Pubic lice (pediculosis pubis or crab lice) are very tiny insects that infest the pubic hair and survive by feeding on human blood. These parasites are most often spread by sexual contact; in a few cases, they may be picked up through contact with infested bedding or clothing. An estimated 3 million people with new cases of the infestation are treated each year in the United States.

Symptoms. The primary symptom of infestation is itching in the pubic area. Scratching may spread the lice to other parts of the body; thus, every effort should be made to avoid touching the infected area, although this may be difficult.

Diagnosis. Pubic lice are diagnosed easily because they are visible to the naked eye. They are pinhead size, oval in shape, and grayish, but appear reddish-brown when full of blood from their host. Nits, the tiny white eggs, are also visible and are usually observed clinging to the base of pubic hair.

Treatment. Lotions and shampoos that will kill pubic lice are available both over the counter and by prescription. Creams or lotions containing lindane, a powerful pesticide, are most frequently prescribed for the treatment of pubic lice. Pregnant women may be advised not to use this drug, and a physician's recommendations for use in infants and small children should be followed carefully. Itching may persist even after the lice have been eradicated. This is because the skin has been irritated and requires time to heal. A soothing lotion such as calamine may offer temporary relief.

Prevention. All persons with whom an infested individual has come into close contact, including family and close friends as well as sex partners, should be treated to ensure that the lice have been eliminated. In addition, all clothing and bedding should be dry cleaned or washed in very hot water (125°F), dried at a high setting, and ironed to rid them of any lice. Pubic lice die within 24 hours of being separated from the body. Because the eggs may live up to 6 days, it is important to apply the treatment for the full time recommended.

Scabies

Scabies is a skin infestation with a tiny mite, Sarcoptes scabiei. Scabies has become relatively common throughout the general population. It is highly contagious and is spread primarily through sexual contact, although it also is commonly transmitted by contact with skin, infested sheets, towels, or even furniture.

Symptoms. Scabies causes intense itching, which often becomes worse at night. Small red bumps or lines appear on the body at sites where the female scabies mite has burrowed into the skin to lay her eggs. The areas most commonly affected include the hands (especially between the fingers), wrists, elbows, lower abdomen, and genitals. The skin reaction may not develop until a month or more after infestation. During this time, a person may pass the disease unknowingly to a sex partner or to another person with whom he or she has close contact.

Diagnosis. Scabies may be confused with other skin irritations such as poison ivy or eczema. To make an accurate diagnosis, a doctor takes a scraping of the irritated area and examines it under a microscope, to reveal the presence of the mite.

Treatment. As with pubic lice, lindane is an effective treatment for scabies. Pregnant women should consult a doctor before using this product. Nonprescription remedies such as sulfur ointment also are available. Sulfur is fairly effective but may be objectionable because of its odor and messiness. Itching can persist even after the infestation has been eliminated because of lingering skin irritation. A hydrocortisone cream or ointment or a soothing lotion may provide relief from itching.

Prevention. Family members and sex partners of a person with scabies are advised to undergo treatment. Twenty-four hours after drug therapy, a person with scabies infestation is no longer contagious to others, even though the skin irritation may persist for some time. As with pubic lice, special care must be taken to rid clothing and bedding of any mites.

The 10 leading states or territories reporting the highest number of AIDS cases among residents are as follows:

TEN STATES/TERRITORIES REPORTING HIGHEST NUMBER OF AIDS CASES

STATE/TERRITORY	# Of AIDS CASES
New York	136,062
California	115,366
Florida	75,539
Texas	51,449
New Jersey	40,216
Puerto Rico	23,546
Illinois	23,220
Pennsylvania	22,988
Georgia	21,628
Maryland	20,231

AIDS CASES BY AGE

AGE	# Of AIDS CASES
Under 5:	6,753
Ages 5 to 12:	1,965
Ages 13 to 19:	3,725
Ages 20 to 24:	25,904
Ages 25 to 29:	97,675
Ages 30 to 34:	164,989
Ages 35 to 39:	164,076
Ages 40 to 44:	120,541
Ages 45 to 49:	69,546
Ages 50 to 54:	36,686
Ages 55 to 59:	20,251
Ages 60 to 64:	11,258
Ages 65 or older:	10,002

What is HIV?

HIV was discovered in 1983. HIV is a retrovirus that infects several kinds of cells in the body, the most important of which is a type of white blood cell called the CD4 lymphocyte (also known as "T-cell") .

> **Human Immunodeficiency Virus**
>
> Is the virus that causes AIDS.

The CD4 cell is a major component of the human immune system that helps keep people free from many infections and some cancers. HIV can effectively disable the body's immune system, and destroy its ability to fight diseases.

Two major types of HIV have been identified so far:

- HIV-1 is the cause of the worldwide epidemic.

- HIV-2 is found mostly in Africa.

- At least ten different sub-types of HIV-1 have also been found.

HIV infection is spread through exposure to semen and vaginal fluid (including menstrual blood) from unprotected sex (without a condom) or through exposure to blood from injection drug use (via contaminated needles or syringes). HIV can also be transmitted from mother to child through birth or by breast feeding.

> **AIDS** stands for Acquired Immunodeficiency Syndrome.

References

1. Institute of Medicine. Committee on Prevention and Control of Sexually Transmitted Diseases. *The Hidden Epidemic: Confronting Sexually Transmitted Diseases*. Eng TR and Butler WT, eds. Washington, DC: National Academy Press, 1997.

2. Centers for Disease Control and Prevention. Summary of notifiable diseases in the United States, 1996. *MMWR* 1997;45:1-103.

3. World Health Organization. *Global Prevalence and Incidence of Selected Curable Sexually Transmitted Diseases: Overview and Estimates*. Geneva: WHO, 1996.

4. World Bank. *World Development Report, 1993: Investing in Health*. New York: Oxford University Press,

5. UNAIDS: Report on the Global HIV/AIDS Epidemic, December, 1997.

6. World Health Organization. *World Health Report 1997*. Geneva: WHO 1997.

7. Centers for Disease Control and Prevention. National Center for HIV, STD and TB Prevention. *Sexually Transmitted Disease Surveillance 1996*. Atlanta: CDC 1997.

8. Westrom L, *et al*. Pelvic inflammatory disease and fertility. A cohort of 1,844 women with laparoscopically verified disease and 657 control women with normal laparoscopic results. *Sex Transm Dis* 1992;19:185-92.

9. Fleming DT, et al. Herpes Simplex Virus type 2 in the United States, 1976 to 1994. *NEJM* 1997;337:1105-11.